THE NEW SCIENCE LITERACY

Using Language Skills to Help Students Learn Science

MARLENE THIER
with
BENNETT DAVISS

Foreword by
HAROLD PRATT

HEINEMANN
Portsmouth, NH

Heinemann
A division of Reed Elsevier Inc.
361 Hanover Street
Portsmouth, NH 03801-3912
www.heinemann.com

Offices and agents throughout the world

The authors and publisher wish to thank those who have generously given permission to reprint borrowed material:

Henry Holt & Co. for permission to reprint "Birches," from *The Poetry of Robert Frost,* edited by Edward Connery Latham, copyright 1969 by Henry Holt and Company, LLC. Reprinted by permission of Henry Holt and Company, LLC.

The writing of this book was supported in part by the National Science Foundation through the Issue-Oriented Elementary Science Leadership grant (IOESL), a teacher enhancement grant #ESI-9554163. Ideas and opinions expressed are those of the authors and not necessarily those of the foundation.

Library of Congress Cataloging-in-Publication Data
Thier, Marlene.
  The new science literacy : using language skills to help students learn
science / Marlene Thier with Bennett Daviss ; foreword by Harold Pratt.
      p. cm.
  Includes bibliographical references (p. 180) and index.
  ISBN 0-325-00459-5 (pbk. : alk. paper)
    1. Science—Study and teaching (Elementary)—United States.   2. Science—Study
and teaching (Secondary)—United States.   3. Language arts (Elementary)—
United States.   4. Language arts (Secondary)—United States.   5. Language arts—
Correlation with content subjects—United States.   I. Daviss, Bennett.   II. Title.

LB1585.3 .T487   2002
507.1—dc21   2001007441

Editor: Robin Najar
Production: Vicki Kasabian
Cover design: Lisa Fowler
Typesetter: TechBooks
Manufacturing: Steve Bernier

Printed in the United States of America on acid-free paper
06   05   04   03   02   VP   1   2   3   4   5

To Herb

This book is dedicated to my husband, Herb, who has encouraged me by his challenge to follow my vision, be strong in my purpose, and never waiver in my resolve to articulate my message clearly. He has been my mentor, my supporter, willing to listen, eager to learn, and helpful beyond belief. My love always and forever to my best friend. Thank you for being you.

Marlene

Contents

PART 1   THE NEW SCIENCE LITERACY: WHAT IT IS AND WHY WE NEED IT

PART 2   HOW TO IMPLEMENT THE NEW SCIENCE LITERACY IN THE CLASSROOM

PART 3   WHAT THE NEW SCIENCE LITERACY MEANS IN THE CLASSROOM AND BEYOND

If the purpose of teaching is to promote learning, then we need to ask what we mean by the term. Here I become passionate. I want to talk about learning. But not the lifeless, sterile, futile, quickly forgotten stuff that is crammed into the mind of the poor helpless individual tied into his seat by the iron-clad bonds of conformity! I am talking about *learning*—the insatiable curiosity that drives the adolescent boy to absorb everything he can see or hear or read about gasoline engines in order improve the speed and efficiency of his "cruiser." I am talking about the student who says, "I am discovering, drawing in from the outside, and making that which is drawn in a real part of me." I am talking about any learning in which the experience of the learner progresses along this line: "No, no, that's not what I want"; "Wait! This is closer to what I am interested in, what I need"; "Ah, there it is! Now I am grasping and comprehending what I need and what I want to know!"

—Carl Rogers, *Freedom to Learn*

The New Science Literacy

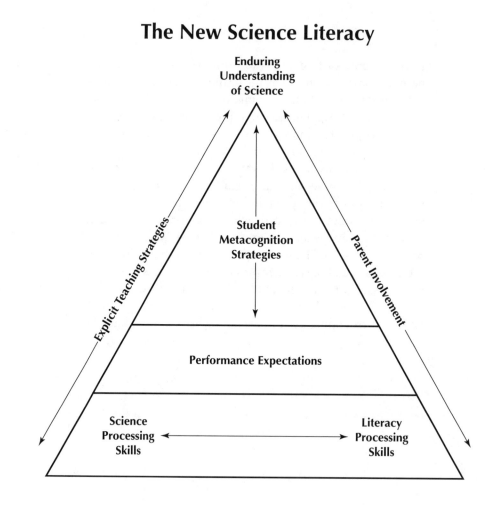

Foreword

The importance of science in the education of all students, including young elementary-age children, is not debatable. How to realize it seems to be. Science rarely is considered basic in the education of elementary students. Recently, with the increasing pressure to be accountable for literacy skills at the elementary level—and, to a lesser degree, at the middle level—teachers are being forced to minimize, if not eliminate, science instruction to make room for an increased emphasis on the teaching of literacy.

In contrast to the decision to forego science instruction, creative teachers and schools at all grade levels are searching for ways to integrate the teaching of science with literacy instruction. The conscientious ones are sometimes painfully aware that such attempts are not all straightforward. In *The New Science Literacy*, Marlene Thier and Bennett Daviss overcome this dilemma and confusion by providing clear guidance and concrete examples of how to link science and language instruction by demonstrating the inherent interdependence of the two disciplines.

Although the book stresses the interdependence of science and literacy, it also preserves and enhances the integrity of science as a means of learning through inquiry. The book places the development of language literacy in the context of inquiry-based, activity-oriented science instruction, called for in the *National Science Education Standards*. The standards clearly state that inquiry draws upon information sources and requires a variety of communications media:

> Inquiry is a multifaceted activity that involves making observations; posing questions; examining books and other sources of information to see what is already known; planning investigations; reviewing what is known in light of experimental evidence; using tools to gather, analyze, and interpret data; proposing answers, explanations, and predictions; and communicating the results. (National Research Council 1996)

This emphasis on literacy as an integral part of inquiry is in marked contrast to most efforts to assist teachers in the integration of science and literacy instruction. Too often the means of integration is simply the inclusion of a variety of readings related to the topic of the current science unit. *The New Science Literacy* embraces the richness and usefulness of language as a germane aspect of students' science learning experiences.

The book combines the two disciplines in a practical and useful way with abundant examples, teaching strategies, and blackline masters that help make the sometimes-complex topic of integration concrete and understandable. The practical nature of this book is complemented by a number of research findings that validate the premise that fusing the two disciplines will increase student achievement in both areas. Research cited in the book and elsewhere has developed a strong case for literacy-enhanced, inquiry-based science instruction that develops deep understanding on the part of the student.

One of the ways teachers can enhance the development of deep understanding by their students is by specifying clear, explicit performance expectations in both disciplines that should be achieved from the instruction. To make the role of expectations clear and functional to the reader, *The New Science Literacy* provides an appendix with concise lists of student performance expectations and teaching strategies for achieving them.

An added feature, not found in most works of this nature, is a well-developed set of procedures for organizing a family science night that brings parents and children together in a delightful example of integrating science and literacy in the home and school settings.

Teachers of science and literacy at all levels will gain from reading this helpful book.

Harold Pratt
President, 2001–2002
National Science Teachers Association

Acknowledgments

It is the supreme art of the teacher to awaken joy in creative expression and knowledge.

—ALBERT EINSTEIN

I owe my greatest thanks to you, the teachers who toil endlessly, cleverly thwarting the slings and arrows that assail your dedication and threaten your professionalism. When I talk with you, you remain upbeat and positive in the face of myriad challenges to your professional and personal well-being, including those that the current accountability movement poses. When I visit your classrooms, I see you continue your quest for that glimmer of understanding in your students' eyes—the moment of that great "aha" of complete knowing, the moment when a new understanding has clicked into place in their minds.

It is to you that I offer a deep and abiding "thank you" for sharing your joys and challenges with me. This sharing has become the beam of light that has guided me on this path.

I also am especially grateful to the teachers, administrators, and parents whose strong voices contributed to this book. Your powerful sharing of ideas and your experiences in fusing science and literacy have helped me know that this can happen in the real world. You have grounded my vision in reality and your voices are an inspiration for our profession.

To all of the teachers and other educational leaders who became part of our Issue Oriented Elementary Science Teacher Leadership family, I will remember you always for the many wonderful insights and ideas you showed me when you allowed me to come into your classrooms. IOESL is the very foundation of this book, the program in which my ideas about literacy were germinated through integration.

To my colleagues at the Lawrence Hall of Science and the SEPUP family past and present, I say this: You are true scientists because you have listened to my ideas and tried them out, even when they were still forming and evolving.

xi

You have given me the context and the place to develop and bring these ideas to fruition.

Last but not least, I thank Ben Daviss, my collaborative writer. You have been "word perfect" and undaunted in your quest to help me find just the right language to tell this story. Your sense of humor and your modest presence have been my listening ear as I have attempted to lure you into my web of ideas. My appreciation goes out to you, my newfound friend, for contributing mightily to the essence of this book.

Introduction

*Plutarch said it centuries ago: "Education is not the filling of a bucket.
It is the lighting of a fire."*

This book is a practical manual for educators who teach science to students in grades 4 through 10. It shows teachers how they can link language literacy and science to strengthen students' achievements in both, and it explains the advantages of doing so. The book includes examples of classroom-based activities that teachers can use to meld the two disciplines and lists of explicit performance expectations that both teachers and students can use to guide and assess students' growth in the use of language through science activities.

The theme of this book is that to do good science, one must possess strong language abilities. The book shows that the two subjects call upon reciprocal sets of skills that combine naturally to strengthen students' mastery of science and language at the same time. It also provides detailed teaching strategies rooted in the principles of guided inquiry, a strategy that takes students beyond activity for its own sake and equips them with metacognitive skills that help them plan and guide their own learning toward what Wiggins and McTighe (1998) call "enduring understanding."

We see this integral relationship between science and language reflected in standards now being promulgated in both disciplines, from the National Science Education Standards to the range of new language standards and frameworks that states are establishing. These standards show those who teach science at any grade level that they can combine the two disciplines in activity-centered, inquiry-based science activities that will help strengthen students' achievement in both areas.

Teachers are rightly cautious, even skeptical, about adopting new approaches and methods without having evidence that the innovations will work. For that reason, I have included a chapter that shows readers how other teachers already are successfully combining science and language in their classroom science programs (see Chapter 9). The chapter also directly addresses teachers' common concerns about fusing science and literacy by letting those who have done so tell their stories.

One Educator's Journey

That chapter, like the rest of this book, is the result of my journey as an educator through two worlds—the world of language and the world of science. I now stand between these two worlds, and it has become my quest to show others where the two naturally coincide and how they enhance and extend each other.

I began the journey many years ago when, as a recent college graduate, I became a sixth-grade teacher in East Meadow, New York. Early on, I realized that I could not teach science from the dusty old textbooks piled high on one side of the room; nor did I want to teach language from the dusty old language books piled in another part of the room. I decided that I would combine the two disciplines using readily available materials from the environment, because there was no money for any kind of supplementary materials.

I started with a simple collection of leaves that students had gathered outside beneath our classroom window. Not knowing exactly what I was doing, I asked them to simply look at it and then describe what they saw to a partner. The partner, in turn, was to use another sense, such as touch or smell, and describe his perceptions to his partner. Next, the students generated an array of ideas and questions regarding the leaves. Many aspects of the experience took on a life of their own: the oral language generated written descriptions and the questions became fodder for students' research and further exploration.

My leaf lesson brought my curriculum alive with activity as students began to develop their own collaborative communities. They shared the excitement of their discoveries through exploratory speech, listening to one another, reading for more information, and writing their ideas in reports and formally presenting them to one another. Students were engaged in what they were doing—even those with learning difficulties or who were otherwise unmotivated. It seemed as if there was a life force moving students toward learning, motivated by the desire to know. Throughout, language was the pane of glass through which I could view their thinking, to borrow Emmitt and Pollack's analogy.

Looking back, I realize now that I was using inquiry-based science strategies with language as the vehicle for communication of the students' observations, questions, and continued exploration.

Several years later, the development of the Science Curriculum Improvement Study helped me find new ways to use science as a vehicle to improve students' language. (It influenced me strongly, in part because one of SCIS's key developers was an integral part of my life—my husband, Herb Thier.) I found in SCIS language opportunities for elementary students embedded in activity-based, inquiry-oriented, and developmentally appropriate science materials. In fact, some early forms of SCIS activities were field-tested on our own children, who became lovingly known as "SCIS kids." Years later, when SCIS was being revised, I contributed to the program's more explicit literacy dimension by helping its developers incorporate a student journal. Keeping the journal gave students the opportunity to write and read reflectively about their science experiences, using language to structure their understandings.

I realize now that these early experiences shaped everything I would do later and influenced my concepts of what effective teaching is.

Later, when I entered the field of special education and worked with learning disabled students, I turned again to science—not only to motivate my students, but also as a vehicle to develop their perceptual skills and language abilities. Even in helping eighth-grade boys learn to read, I focused on science as a platform and tool of literacy. Science never failed me. It captivated, it motivated, it engaged, it gave meaning, and it offered the greatest potential in the most diverse situations for the most diverse learners.

Without realizing it, I was creating what Don Holdaway in his book *The Foundations of Literacy* calls "an effective learning environment for the acquisition of literacy" that "should be alive with activity which is felt to be deeply purposeful in all the ways of human meaning" (1979, 14). My students' learning always began with an immersion in an environment in which "the skill [language] was being used in purposeful ways," as Holdaway puts it (14).

In addition, my students were learning language skills not through exercises and drills, but by doing. That underscored for me the reasons that I had shifted my emphasis from "reading for the sake of learning to read" to "reading about something meaningful while learning to read." I knew the process of reading is important, but through my "leaf curriculum," I was able to demonstrate that the skills of language can be acquired within the context of the meaningful ideas of science. I had been heeding the warning that "by emphasizing the process to the exclusion of meaningful ideas, we sacrifice the raison d'etre for learning to read" (Kovalik 1993). Using language naturally, my students internalized science concepts because they were engaged by the power of inquiry.

Strangely enough, when I talked about these ideas with colleagues in the world of language and literacy, they began to listen. Many were even willing to try some of the activities in their own teaching. Attempting the same conversations in the science world—particularly with teachers in middle and high school—was a harder road to travel. Many science teachers felt ill-equipped to teach in language-related fields. Many times I would hear the same words echoing in my ears: "I'm a science teacher. I'm not a literacy teacher. Sure, I think this is important, but it's the job of the language department." Listening to these words, I realized that this was not an outright rejection of my ideas, but rather a plea for help. I believe that these teachers, beneath their words, were saying that they did not know how to do this efficiently within the context of science.

Thus my challenge in writing this book has been twofold: first, to show colleagues from both worlds that the skills and processes of science and literacy are reciprocal and complementary and, second, to show those skeptical teachers—and all of us involved in science education—how we can become more effective teachers of literacy skills within the context of our subject matter of expertise.

Planning for a Different Future

All teachers need to understand that, as John Dewey once put it, "if we teach today as we taught yesterday, we rob our children of tomorrow."

There was a time when transferring facts from textbook to student was the sole objective of science teaching. In those days, a superficial understanding of science concepts probably sufficed. (Indeed, our culture seems to be fascinated by factoids—discrete pieces of unrelated information that are the stock-in-trade of popular television quiz shows.) But does possession of a mental bag of facts make a truly knowledgeable person? Does being educated mean that one knows small pieces of information in many fields, each retrievable at a moment's notice? Or does it mean that one not only can regurgitate facts but also is able to integrate knowledge into a meaningful whole?

I submit that we need to nurture strategic learners who can sort, analyze, compare, contrast, synthesize, infer, apply, make decisions, and use information meaningfully in their lives. Understanding science—being able to use it to make informed personal and societal decisions and having the literacy skills to communicate and learn concepts—is what the new science literacy is about.

Purposes of the Book

Toward that end, this book has four goals:

1. to demonstrate to every science educator that linking science and language education strengthens students' knowledge and skills in both areas because the disciplines are inherently interdependent;

2. to demonstrate to science educators that the natural synergies between language and science make the work of linking the two disciplines not only worthwhile but also easier to accomplish than many teachers might think, especially when used within a context of guided inquiry;

3. to provide specific strategies, techniques, and lists of student performance expectations that can help teachers fuse science and language experiences to synergize students' learning about science, language, and themselves; and

4. to help those who teach science and their students to broaden their repertoire of intellectual skills. If students are better able to think scientifically and express themselves effectively, they will learn and achieve more in a variety of content areas. This can help students and teachers meet the challenges posed by the growing use of standardized tests.

In addition, I believe there are seven urgent needs in science education to which the concept of fusing science and language can make a unique contribution.

Strengthening the place of science in the curriculum

Despite the advent of the National Science Education Standards in 1996, the place of science in the elementary curriculum is in jeopardy. Teachers and administrators, pressured by the growing use of high-stakes standardized tests in math and reading, can too easily channel resources—from class time to materials budgets—into those two areas and away from science and other disciplines. But by linking science and language literacy, science educators can demonstrate the role of science in strengthening students' language skills, thus extending and strengthening the place of science in a basic curriculum.

Helping elementary teachers

Elementary teachers new to the profession often lack a firm grounding in science content. Indeed, many elementary teachers are as uncomfortable teaching science as they are comfortable teaching language skills. These teachers are the most likely to lack clear ideas about how to blend language and science education.

By joining language skills to the content and processes of science, elementary teachers can use what they know well to broaden their teaching abilities. The ideas and methods in this book also can enable them to capitalize on science's rich content as a venue for helping students both learn about the physical world and express their learning through language. Also, as a supervisor of student teachers, I find that too many elementary teachers enter their profession without as firm a foundation as they think they have in the skills of teaching the mechanics of reading. This can be especially true among teachers entering the profession in midlife or under emergency certification. These teachers can more quickly develop their skills and gain confidence in teaching reading and science by leveraging the two disciplines' sets of reciprocal skills.

Helping teachers in the upper grades

Science teachers in middle and high schools are, for the most part, science specialists. They do not expect (and should not be expected) also to be English teachers. Instead, they usually assume that their students arrive in science classrooms with an adequate ability to extract meaning from language within the context of science. However, as all science teachers know, a significant number of students cannot.

Research shows that the problem is not a lack of decoding skills, but weak comprehension—an inability to accurately grasp the meaning of what is read (Schoenbach et al. 1999). When students are unable to comprehend the meanings embodied in language, science instruction is likely to be dramatically less effective than if students possess strong language skills. The techniques presented in this book address this comprehension problem specifically and directly and show science teachers various approaches they can use to help their students overcome it. The methods emphasize limited teacher intervention and highlight ways in which teachers can help students guide their own learning.

The good news is that science offers endless opportunities for students to practice using language clearly and precisely. By learning some simple techniques, and by providing students with some self-help skills detailed in this book, science teachers can foster the growth of those skills in their students and, as a result, teach science more effectively.

Enhancing the movements for accountability, standards, and educational improvement

It is a fact of life that the national movement for educational improvement increasingly emphasizes teachers' accountability for students' achievements. (I do not object in principle to this linkage, but I do have some sharp disagreements with many of the ways in which it is being implemented.) At the same time, the advent of national standards for science and language literacy are setting new guidelines for instructional programs.

As stated earlier, this book shows teachers in elementary, middle, and high school how to use language literacy and science to strengthen each other in the classroom and thereby boost students' achievement in both subjects. In elementary grades, science draws on children's natural curiosity about the world to provide a rich context for language instruction. In upper grades, students learn science better as their command of language enables them to better comprehend what they read and to use evidence and language together to arrive at decisions and conclusions.

Preparing a scientifically literate population

As citizens as well as workers, tomorrow's adults will need to effectively apply a range of scientific skills and knowledge to understand their world and communicate about it. That demands a set of skills that marries a knowledge of science facts, concepts, and processes with the ability to use language clearly and precisely to comprehend, articulate, and communicate about scientific issues and ideas. How do we as a society address the issue of global warming? Should you take antioxidant tablets? Is food irradiation dangerous or beneficial?

The introduction to the *National Science Education Standards* declares that the standards "are designed to guide our nation toward a scientifically literate society," in part because "Americans are confronted increasingly with questions in their lives that require scientific information and scientific ways of thinking for informed decision making" (National Research Council 1996). This book can help educators prepare students to answer those questions effectively.

Improving students' performance on standardized tests

The efficacy of standardized tests and testing regimes remains a matter of debate, but the tests themselves have become a fact of life for teachers and students. The principal purpose of fusing language and science is *not* merely to raise students' scores on standardized tests. However, schools and districts using these strategies find that the combination often helps raise students' test scores in both science and language. (Research shows correlations as high as 0.9 between students' scores on standardized tests in reading and science.) With teachers' performance evaluations increasingly tied to their students' scores on standardized tests (another fact of life with which I take issue), this feature alone may interest a number of teachers in learning more about the strategies this book presents.

Helping special-needs students

Fusing literacy and science in an inquiry-based curriculum that students find relevant to their own lives is good teaching practice, and good teaching practice benefits all students. But I have found that many of these strategies for combining a greater emphasis on language with activity-based science are especially effective in helping ESL, LD, and other students with special needs learn and retain more—in language skills and in science.

According to the National Alliance of Business, about 30 percent of U.S. students now come from minority groups. That number is projected to rise to 37 percent by 2015. The U.S. Department of Education reports that in Alaska, New Mexico, and California, more than 20 percent of all students have limited English proficiency. That number rises to 45 percent in the Los Angeles school district and more than 25 percent in Houston's schools.

Those numbers make the concepts and techniques that this book presents especially useful now and even more so in the years ahead.

Why This Book Is Unique

Although other books address the combination of science and language in the classroom, this book is different from them in several ways.

First, other authors addressing the combination of language and science concentrate almost entirely on reading and writing. Partly as a result, many teachers' notion of "literacy in science" is assigning students to read trade books related to the theme of the science topic they currently are studying. This practice is rampant, but it is also limiting. In contrast, this book defines *literacy* to mean not only reading and writing but also speaking, listening, and media analysis. As a result, it discusses teaching strategies and performance expectations for areas that other books in the field largely ignore.

Second, the ideas and techniques in this book have evolved from my continuing, original work in using language skills to improve science learning. I have personally created or adapted many of the ideas and techniques explained in the book, used them with teachers, and refined them in classrooms. Teachers, schools, and many urban districts are using some of the methods explained in this book to improve students' learning in science.

Third, this book places language literacy in the context of inquiry-based, activity-oriented science. This framework for science education, mandated by the National Science Education Standards, embraces the richness of language as a fundamental aspect of students' science experiences. Inquiry-based science is gaining ground in a curricular landscape still dominated by the conventional textbook-and-lecture approach to learning. This book highlights the vital role that language plays in effective inquiry-based science.

Fourth, the book highlights the importance of metacognition—helping students become aware of and structure their own thought processes. This in itself is a newly emerging approach to teaching. Metacognitive teaching techniques let all students in on the secrets that the best learners know and use intuitively. Therefore, the book can help teachers show students how to help themselves learn science while using language more effectively.

Fifth, not all books in this area are written for teachers' practical use. This book is. It includes practical teaching strategies that unite science and language and explicit performance expectations that teachers can use to track students' progress in using language to learn science better. In a special section, the book also addresses in frank terms teachers' skepticism about linking science and language, as well as success stories where these strategies were implemented.

A Shared Journey

It is my hope that, as teachers see value in these approaches, they will not only use the methods and activities as they are described but also adapt them to their own needs or use them as inspirations to create their own lessons. This book is not an attempt to suggest that one size fits all. Instead, I have tried to create a set of resource materials that will stimulate thinking so that teachers can nip and tuck and make a given activity or technique a "perfect fit" for their own classrooms; or, perhaps these suggestions will simply inspire teachers to create their own unique set of ideas and strategies for fusing science and literacy. If that is the case, then I shall feel truly successful because teachers themselves will have created the perfect set of resources.

It also is my hope that teachers will share their own strategies with the rest of us to enlighten our thinking as we journey down this path to greater understanding together.

1

Merging Science and Language

The important thing is to not stop questioning.
—ALBERT EINSTEIN

In an age fueled by information and driven by technology, understanding the concepts and processes of science is as indispensable as knowing how to read, write, speak, and listen. As citizens and as workers, adults in the twenty-first century will need to effectively apply a range of scientific skills and knowledge to understand their world and communicate about it.

In other words, they will need to be scientifically literate—to possess a set of skills that marries knowledge of science concepts, facts, and processes with the ability to use language to articulate and communicate about ideas. The *National Science Education Standards* declares in its introduction that the standards "are designed to guide our nation toward a scientifically literate society" in part because "Americans are confronted increasingly with questions in their lives that require scientific information and scientific ways of thinking for informed decision making" (National Research Council 1996).

This new, central role of science in our everyday lives places new demands on educators. All students, not just a gifted few, must now learn not only how science works but also how to apply the principles and processes of science in their daily lives as workers, citizens, and consumers. Educators are being called upon to ensure that students internalize scientific habits of mind, such as using evidence to separate opinion from fact. If students are to become adults capable of making informed choices and taking effective action, then educators must make sure that students absorb those habits into their regular

1

patterns of thought so that those habits stay with students long after their time in school has ended.

At the same time, the new importance of science opens a new opportunity for educators. It enables us to merge the teaching of science and the teaching of language literacy to strengthen students' skills in, and mastery of, both. As Johanna Scott (1992) writes in the introduction to her book *Science and Language Links,* "Language plays [roles] in science learning . . . science can be used to develop children's language, and . . . increased knowledge of language goes hand in hand with the development of scientific ideas." Researchers have found that students learn science better when they write about their thinking and that the act of writing "may force integration of new ideas and relationships with prior knowledge. This forced integration may also provide feedback to the writer and encourage personal involvement" with what is being studied (Fellows 1994).

In the classroom, science and language become interdependent, in part because each is based on processes and skills that are mirrored in the other. These reciprocal skills give teachers and students a unique leverage: by fusing science and language in the classroom, teachers can help students learn both more effectively. Moreover, teachers can do so without taking on undue additional burdens to their work time or professional education.

They can do so by coordinating three approaches. The first is to share with students specific **performance expectations** that let students understand what excellence "looks like" and the steps they need to take to achieve it. The second is to empower students with strategies of **metacognition**—techniques that enable students to become aware of their own habits of thought while learning. When they become aware of their own thought processes, students can take steps to alter them and make them more effective and efficient. Third, teachers can use performance expectations and student metacognitive skills to design **strategies for explicit teaching** that show students exactly how to apply and cultivate the two methods of self-help. In the following chapters, readers will learn how to combine the three approaches to shift the locus of classroom effort and engagement from the teacher to students, a shift that can relieve teachers of a significant instructional burden.

The suggestion that teachers can link literacy and science to strengthen each other is not one that I make lightly. As a former classroom teacher, and as someone who now works with classroom teachers who teach science, I understand the constraints that teachers face. The school day already is packed full of necessary lessons and activities. Schools' budgets and other resources—especially teachers' time and energy—already are stretched to the limit.

It is here that using literacy and science together can pay educational dividends for students as well as personal dividends for teachers. As a young teacher, I always was willing to incorporate a steady stream of innovations into my personal teaching program because the innovations always seemed valuable. But as the pressures of time began to close in, two problems became clear: while much of value was being added, nothing was taken away. In addition, there was no clear way to combine or synergize different aspects of the expanding program. Using literacy to strengthen science can help teachers accomplish more within the limitations that the clock and the calendar now impose.

I also do not suggest that middle and high school science teachers become English teachers. I do maintain that science educators in the upper grades can find myriad opportunities to support and strengthen the skills and processes of literacy as they teach those of science and that elementary-grade teachers can find just as many opportunities to teach the skills of science while they teach the skills of literacy.

That is not a theoretical statement. We already are seeing educators fuse the two in schools across the United States. As only one example, in New York City elementary classrooms students are lining their classroom walls with stories and poems about their experiments. As part of their literacy learning, students then can "read the room" to strengthen their understanding of science while they practice their reading.

This is only one example. Today's inquiry-oriented, activity-based science courses and lessons present countless opportunities for teachers to use science and literacy to strengthen each other. In the course of their work in inquiry-based science, students regularly

- read and follow instructions on data sheets;
- read and understand informational texts and literary works related to science themes or topics;
- develop analytical skills to make judgments about the sources and reliability of information;
- listen acutely to clearly understand and interpret information given orally;
- participate in cooperative learning groups where speaking and listening skills are the primary means of sharing information, expressing and communicating responses and analysis, and coordinating activities with other group members;
- speak to explain their understandings or points of view about a subject; and
- write journal entries, data sheets, narrative procedures, reports, persuasive documents, and occasionally even creative stories related to their science investigations.

In each of these activities, teachers can enlist a range of language skills to strengthen students' mastery of science. Indeed, the ability to absorb and exchange ideas clearly and precisely by writing, speaking, reading, and listening is an embedded expectation of science: good science and good science education are not possible without strong language skills. Fortunately, the opportunities to strengthen science already exist within the activities designed to teach language literacy skills—and, as we have noted, science holds countless opportunities to strengthen students' skills and processes of language.

Reasons to Link Science and Literacy

When teachers take advantage of ready opportunities to unite science and language to strengthen each other, several benefits result.

First, in elementary grades, science gives meaning and purpose to literacy activities by providing a rich field of content that students are naturally curious about—their bodies, the sky, animals, and so on. When literacy skills are linked to science content, students have personal, practical motivation to master language as a tool that can help them answer their questions about the world around them.

Second, the stronger a student's literacy skills, the stronger the student's grasp of science will be. Among people who are not professional scientists, scientific concepts, principles, and information are most easily expressed and understood in nonmathematical terms. Therefore, language becomes the primary avenue that students must travel to arrive at scientific understanding. As Fellows points out, "Writing [enables] students to express their current ideas about scientific topics in a form that they could look at and think about" (1994). Her study found that "written words provided cues for expressing ideas verbally to others. Listening to others' responses and verbal expressions helped them reflect on their previous ideas and evaluate what was useful for making sense. Writing, speaking, and listening provided practice as students constructed new ideas and supplied a rich playground for expressive exploration as students tried out their new conceptions." In that way, a student's achievement in science will be directly proportional to the student's ability to use language.

Third, many, and perhaps most, teachers in middle and high school assume that students entering science courses in the upper grades have an adequate vocabulary and the necessary skills to decode print and draw meaning from language. But too often, this is not the case. Older students may be able to perform the mechanics of reading, but comprehension—particularly in specific content areas—frequently eludes them. By employing a few well-chosen literacy techniques, and by teaching students some self-help skills, science teachers can help students improve their reading comprehension and, therefore, their achievement in science. The techniques and skills are not complicated; they do not require teachers to undergo extensive professional development in order to use them. However, the methods do require a relatively small amount of class time to demonstrate the skills to students and to coach students in using them. Teachers who have done so report that the time they invested has been more than repaid in students' accelerated academic progress and in their increased ability to learn independently, without the repeated teacher intervention and monitoring that often accompanies traditional instructional methods.

Fourth, literacy gives teachers new tools to assess students' science learning. At least one study has found that "analyzing students' narrative writings . . . provided a methodology sensitive to distinguishing changes in students' thinking" (Kleinsasser, Paradis, and Stewart 1992). Another has "demonstrated that student writing provided a vehicle for teachers to follow students' changes in thinking. . . . Students' written ideas provided a window into their thinking processes" (Fellows 1994).

Also, linking science and literacy can help rescue science education from a precarious future. At this writing, science teaching and learning are at risk, especially in elementary grades. In recent years, policymakers and the public have been gripped by the idea that student scores on standardized tests in reading and mathematics must improve year by year. Consequently, in elementary grades other subjects are not infrequently shunted aside as disproportionate amounts of class time are devoted to drills and exercises in math, reading, and test-taking techniques.

In the upper grades, science does not necessarily escape the damage wrought by the pervasive emphasis on standardized tests in language and math. Thanks to those tests, districts have powerful incentives to channel money and other assets disproportionately to those disciplines, robbing science education of the resources it needs to ensure that students learn science effectively.

Science educators can stem that trend by linking literacy and science. By merging the two where possible, teachers can demonstrate that their subject has educational power across the curriculum. By making their subject a key element in strengthening literacy skills, teachers can demonstrate that emphasizing science—not ignoring or de-emphasizing it—is a crucial step in raising students' achievement scores on standardized language exams, currently a dominant aim among thousands of school districts. By reinforcing literacy skills within its own context, science can retain its place in a curriculum that, due to external pressures, too often skews its emphasis toward other disciplines.

The purpose of this book is to help educators tap those vast synergies. In the chapters that follow, teachers will find an arsenal of insights and techniques that they can use to support the goals of literacy as they use inquiry-based science activities to engage and challenge students.

Reciprocal Skills

Tremendous synergies are possible between the disciplines of science and language literacy because, in their essence, they seek to develop reciprocal skills in students—skills that complement and strengthen each other. It is possible to develop those skills in students through science or through language, but either challenge is simplified enormously when the resources of both disciplines are intentionally focused on the same tasks. Science strengthens literacy skills by infusing them with meaning and purpose. Setting language in an engaging context such as science inspires students to reach for the tools of language in order to uncover and internalize the secrets about the world that science can reveal to them. Literacy skills strengthen science learning by giving students the lens of language through which to focus and clarify their ideas, conclusions, inferences, and procedures. By integrating those groups of skills, teachers can improve students' abilities and raise achievement levels in both areas at once, and do so more effectively and efficiently than if the two skill areas are taught separately.

These synergies begin to become clear when one understands everything that the term *literacy* embraces. With that understanding, teachers of science and language can begin to discern the common needs and goals from which the two sets of skills spring. Teachers also can glimpse the territory that they share as educators with common objectives.

In the twenty-first century, literacy embraces all the skills of language, including

- reading, not only to decode print but also to understand, retain, and apply its meanings;
- writing and speaking clearly and concisely enough to be able to clarify one's own thoughts and ideas and to transmit their precise meanings to others;
- listening attentively enough to understand what others really mean when they speak; and
- what has been called "viewing" or "media literacy"—the ability to critically analyze and evaluate the usefulness of information, subtle or hidden meanings within it, and the objectivity of its sources.

The latter is being recognized as a key skill in language arts, but it has long had a place in science. Inherently, science is a process of probing new ideas and statements for weaknesses, flaws, bias, and hidden meanings. Particularly in the upper grades, science courses encourage students to view data with a scientist's skeptical eye, especially now that so much unrefereed information is pouring over the Internet, through media, and from advertising. In developing the skills of media literacy as part of language studies, students learn to dissect advertisements and other, more subtle informational messages to discern bias and hidden meanings. The processes of making such judgments in each discipline are similar. Therefore, the analytical habits of skepticism so essential to science can be developed in either discipline and can strengthen and reinforce the same important skills in the other.

At first glance, the skills of science might not seem similar to those of language. Science demands quantitative skills, while decoding and understanding language has little to do with numbers. But, when one looks deeper, one can see again that the two disciplines are based on a foundation of parallel or reciprocal processes. For example, a scientist at work on an experiment will

- **note the details** of an experiment as the processes unfold;
- **compare and contrast** results achieved under different experimental conditions;
- **predict** the outcome of future experiments by using data from the investigation;
- **sequence events,** both in structuring an experiment and in analyzing its results;
- **link cause and effect** in analyzing the experiment's results;
- **distinguish fact from opinion** in presenting the data;
- **make inferences** and draw conclusions based on what has been observed;
- **use words** in ways that communicate a practical understanding of their meanings; and
- **use language** to communicate experimental results and to interpret their meanings to colleagues clearly and completely enough so that others can attempt to replicate the work and confirm its outcomes.

Compare that list with a list of literacy skills adapted from the New Standards project, a joint venture of the Learning Research and Development Center at the University of Pittsburgh and the National Center for Education and the Economy. These generic skills, adapted specifically for use with inquiry-based science programs, are commonly used as frameworks or guidelines by school districts and materials developers. The skills suggest that students should be able to

- **note details.** Being able to observe and retain the small details of a physical scene or a character's behavior in a story (or even noting the specific letters that a word comprises in order to decode it) calls on the same skills as being able to perceive small details about the physical changes materials undergo in a chemical reaction;
- **compare and contrast,** whether in listening to two public officials' views on the same event or in making notes about the way that a variety of substances react with vinegar;
- **predict,** a skill that calls on the previous two to forecast what will happen next, whether in a science experiment or in the plot of a novel;
- **sequence events,** a skill that taps the same processes of logic and analysis whether students are following step-by-step procedures to conduct a science experiment or compiling clues to solve a mystery story;
- **link cause and effect,** as in discussing what happens when enteric and regular aspirin are dissolved in acidic and base solutions or what causes a character in a story to react to an event in a particular way;
- **distinguish fact from opinion,** a skill that demands the use of evidence in discussing a book or a scientific process (and is especially crucial in analyzing media messages);
- **link words with precise meanings** by learning the meaning of words through experience, either by discovering a word's meaning in the context of a written passage or through a science activity that equips students with an operational definition of a concept instead of an abstract term alien to their personal experiences;
- **make inferences** based on observation and evidence; and
- **draw conclusions** by combining data from various sources, an ability that is a culmination of all of the above skills and processes, both in literacy and in science.

Conclusion: The Interdependence of Science and Literacy

Good science—and effective teaching and learning in science—is dependent upon strong language skills. Indeed, science and language are inextricably linked in the pursuit, determination, and communication of meaning in the context of the physical world.

As an example, consider the deceptively simple question "Is the lake polluted?" What does the question mean? Technically, it asks whether the water contains harmful substances. But which substances? At what concentrations have they been found in the lake? Do those concentrations threaten public or environmental health? According to which studies? Who conducted the studies? Were those studies structured in a valid and unbiased way? Do the levels in the water exceed government-set maximums for those substances? Are those maximums reasonable?

Increasingly, public policy questions require citizens, through their votes or voluntary actions, to decide the answers. To make those decisions, citizens must understand the scientific facts and processes in play, and they must be able to use language to communicate accurately about the scientific information on which those decisions must be based. Making evidence-based decisions about science-related public policy questions in a free society requires a majority of citizens to blend science and language skills, using each to illuminate the other.

Just as language clarifies and communicates the meaning of science, science can strengthen the meanings that students find in language studies. Research has shown that the acquisition of literacy skills is significantly enhanced when those skills are used for specific purposes within a meaningful and stimulating context. Science can provide that effective learning environment, not only in elementary grades but also throughout a student's school career. Language instruction in concert with materials-centered science activities can provide just that purposeful environment needed to reinforce students' emerging literacy skills. At the same time, studies have shown that student learning in science is improved by the introduction of literacy-related activities (Rowe 1996; Bredderman 1983; Fellows 1994; Holliday 1994). As Holliday notes, "Hands-on experiences are necessary, but not sufficient, to learn many counterintuitive science concepts. Likewise, language is necessary, but not sufficient, in initial learning of abstract concepts. The important factors are: what types of thinking and strategies are mutually beneficial in reading, writing, and science?"

In the following chapters, we will begin to answer that question.

2

Activities That Merge Language and Science

Science is not a list of facts and principles to learn by rote. It is a way of looking at the world and asking questions.

—JAMES RUTHERFORD, EDUCATION ADVISER TO THE
AMERICAN ASSOCIATION FOR THE ADVANCEMENT OF SCIENCE

The idea that teachers can actively use the skills of literacy and science to support, strengthen, and enhance each other immediately raises questions among teachers. One of the first is "What exactly would this look like in my classroom?"

The answer, of course, will be different in elementary classrooms than in those of upper grades. As part of their kit of professional tools, elementary teachers are skilled in combining various categories of content with literacy activities. As a result, elementary classrooms usually are rich in language—talking, questioning, storytelling, listening, writing, debating, and, of course, reading for a variety of purposes—as teachers use weather, insects, and other aspects of the physical world to introduce science to children through the lens of language.

But there also is a danger in those opportunities. Elementary teachers often have little background in science; many are uncomfortable teaching science or even intimidated by their limited knowledge of the subject. In those classrooms, science content can too easily be lost in an emphasis on language. "For the most part, the elementary school classroom is a humanities culture," according to education professor Mae Carson Reinhardt (2000, 2). "It is a culture that science specialists sometimes find difficult to enter."

"On the other hand," she points out, if teachers can capitalize on their "strengths in language arts and find new ways to integrate science throughout the curriculum, there might be greater success in bringing more science to elementary school classrooms and in developing comfortable, competent teachers of science" (2). In other words, fusing language and science enables those teachers to broaden their use of effective teaching strategies from other content areas to their science teaching as well. The teachers can use elements with which they already are comfortable to gain the confidence to address a broader range of science content.

In middle and high school, where tradition and sharp organizational lines segregate disciplines, the problem typically is the opposite. Science teachers, particularly in high school, usually have a deeper knowledge of particular scientific disciplines than elementary teachers do. But they often are less aware of the natural relationship between science and language.

In addition, teachers in the upper grades usually assume that students, by the time they begin their middle school years, need no additional strengthening in the use of language and that students have acquired adequate literacy skills to communicate science ideas effectively. However, as many educators know from hard experience, too often that is not the case—but not necessarily for the reason that most teachers think.

When adolescents have difficulty reading in science or other subjects, teachers often assume that the struggling students are unable to decode the words on the page. That often can be true for disadvantaged students. But research shows that typically students "are far less likely to have problems with decoding than with comprehension. These students typically have not [done] much [science content] reading. . . . As a result, they have very little stamina or persistence" (Schoenbach et al. 1999). Students can read the words but cannot as easily extract and link their meanings.

For science teachers facing the problem, this research implies good news. It means that by infusing their science teaching with some readily available tools of literacy, science teachers in upper grades can help these students on the spot. These students need not be remanded to special education or remedial reading classes. (In fact, such dramatic action can be counterproductive, doing additional damage to students' motivation.) Instead, with some easy-to-use literacy techniques, teachers can help these students use science to learn to employ language more effectively while using language to learn science better.

In that way, teachers at every grade level can use science to strengthen students' mastery of language skills. At the same time, they can employ the techniques of literacy to strengthen students' skills and abilities in science. To do so, teachers can use various **literacy performance expectations** (detailed in Chapters 3 through 7) to help them assess students' growth in the use of language to capture and master scientific concepts and skills. The expectations also enable students to understand what direction that growth should take and what is expected of them.

In this chapter, we will offer a few glimpses of how the two disciplines already are being blended in science lessons to improve students' achievement in both areas.

Guided Inquiry in Science Education

The quest to link science and literacy always depends on the creativity and awareness of individual teachers. But teachers are supported in that quest by the approach to science teaching, now gaining a foothold in U.S. schools, known as "guided inquiry" (H. Thier and Daviss 2001). The skills of science and of literacy join naturally in science experiences for students that are structured using the principles of guided inquiry.

After explaining what guided inquiry is, we will explore four inquiry-based activities developed by the Science Education for Public Understanding Program, based at the Lawrence Hall of Science at the University of California at Berkeley. The examples, drawn from a range of grade levels, fuse the skills of science and of literacy in the service of each other.

In science education, *guided inquiry* can be defined as using a series of structured, sequenced scientific investigations that integrate appropriate processes and information (or of activities and rigorous academic content, to use education's preferred terms), chosen through research, to fashion meaningful learning experiences for students. Those experiences are effective when they

- engage students at an emotional level by confronting them with issues or problems that have meaning in students' own lives. Placing scientific ideas and processes in the context of actual issues—balancing the risks and benefits of genetically engineered food, for example—can suddenly give abstract concepts a personal meaning to students, a key element in helping them master knowledge;

- capitalize on students' engagement to lead them to use the concepts, techniques, and information of science to reason their way through a scientific or technological issue and to make an informed personal decision about the issue that is justified by the data or evidence; and

- help students master increasingly sophisticated scientific principles, concepts, methods, and information in ways that will enable them to retain that content beyond a final test.

A feature that distinguishes guided inquiry from conventional hands-on science learning is that, after students complete an assigned activity, they are encouraged to design their own projects and investigations to continue exploring the topic. Through these self-chosen activities (guided and supervised by a teacher), students pursue their own questions about the subject. The additional work helps students link key ideas, rethink their own theories about the topic, and perhaps even satisfy their remaining curiosity about it.

The principles of guided inquiry are based on two ideas, proven by research.

First, students learn better when they experience something by doing it instead of reading about it in a textbook or hearing about it in a lecture. Students retain only 5 percent to 10 percent of what they read in textbooks but can recall as much as 80 percent of the details of something they have experienced (National Training Laboratories n.d.).

This principle expresses the essence of constructivism: When students work like scientists, they use language to organize, recognize, and internalize the concepts, principles, and information that they encounter through activities. Language becomes a scaffold on which students construct their understandings. By providing literacy opportunities for students in science, educators enrich the context for both subjects so students can more effectively expand their personal structures of science knowledge by improving their language skills.

Second, more than two decades of constructivist research show that mastery—the level of learning that our society and economy increasingly demand from each student—is best achieved through engagement (Thier and Daviss 2001). Studies have shown that true learning takes place only when students engage with information and processes deeply enough to weave that content into their personal views and understandings of how the world works (Harlen 2000).

Indeed, teaching and learning based on guided inquiry are squarely at the center of the National Science Education Standards, which call for:

Less emphasis on:	More emphasis on:
knowing scientific facts and information	understanding scientific concepts and developing abilities of inquiry
studying subject matter disciplines for their own sake	learning subject matter disciplines in the context of inquiry; of technology and science; of personal and social perspectives; and of the history and nature of science
separating science knowledge and science processes	integrating all aspects of science content

| implementing inquiry as a set of processes | implementing inquiry as instructional strategies, abilities, and ideas to be learned |

(National Research Council 1996)

Clearly, the concept of guided inquiry gives equal weight to knowledge and skills, slighting neither science facts nor science processes. But it also emphasizes concepts more than rote formulas and emphasizes learning science in a personal and social context instead of as discrete sets of compartmentalized abstractions. To take students beyond the mathematical and formulaic aspects of science, teachers must rely on students' language skills. By embedding an inquiry within both the context of students' lives and strong science content, then sequencing investigations as part of a larger curricular design, educators can reach their curricular and instructional goals for science and for literacy at the same time.

Guided inquiry also provides teachers with an additional way to enlist literacy skills: the kind of embedded, authentic assessment becoming increasingly common in guided inquiry lends itself with relative ease to assessing language skills at the same time. Students read for basic and background information; they read and follow instructions on data sheets. They write reports and narrative procedures, make oral presentations, and engage in classroom discussions and debates. Each activity gives teachers ready opportunities to assess individual students' strengths and weaknesses in the range of language skills against a set of specific performance expectations.

As our definition of guided inquiry implies, we do not suggest that the sole, or even main, reason to merge literacy and science is to enable students to do a better job of reading conventional textbooks. If teachers unite language and science skills in classroom activities, students will read textbooks more effectively, but that is not the goal. The goal of fusing literacy and science is to strengthen students' abilities to combine science and literacy in processing evidence to reach, then express and communicate, personal knowledge, understanding, and decisions about the world around them. Fusing literacy with science through guided inquiry gives students the tools of language, and therefore of thought, to represent their understandings of the activity itself as well as the scientific concepts, information, and processes that they have learned through the activity. Articulating their experiences and conclusions clarifies their thinking. As Emmitt and Pollock put it, "Language is a pane of glass through which we can view our thinking" (1991).

It is important to remember that guided inquiry has a place in literacy skills as well. For example, when helping students learn to help themselves, teachers often find it useful to teach students to ask explicit questions about a work before they read it. From the title, what would you expect the work to be about? Why does the author make this particular statement or claim? What will happen next? As students become aware of their own expectations and responses to a work, they can use their ongoing questions and answers to focus their reading and make it meaningful to them. Huber and Walker (1996) found this technique distinctly effective in helping students increase their comprehension.

Guided Inquiry, Literacy, and Special-Needs Students

Children are born with a drive to make sense of the world. As Wells puts it, they are "active seekers of meaning. . . . It does not take young children long to learn that language is the medium that human beings use to construct and reconstruct meaning" (1986). But he also points out that "the emphasis has been on language learning but not learning through language. However, in practice, the two are, to a very considerable degree, co-extensive. . . . Just as children learn the language system through experience [and by] using it as a resource, so in increasing their control of the resources of language they also increase their understanding of the experience" (Wells and Nicholls 1985).

Much of a child's early learning occurs through linguistic interactions with parents and others. Students with special needs or from deprived backgrounds often have not had those necessary experiences. For those students, experiences in school can capitalize on the child's curiosity to expand the child's universe. One of the most effective ways to do that is through the exploratory talk that accompanies collaborative activities in guided inquiry. In that way, children figure out for themselves how language conveys meaning and how to use language to construct their personal understandings of the world. The responsibility of the teacher is to be a facilitator of language: the teacher arranges and maintains optimum conditions within which students enhance their language skills. Inquiry-based science provides an environment for learning both science and language.

As Harlen puts it, "The ideas that we form from direct experience have to be communicated and this involves trying to find words that convey our meaning to others. In this process, our own ideas often have to be reformulated in ways that are influenced by the meaning that others give to words . . . an important element of learning is 'negotiated meaning'" (2000). Through guided inquiry's vehicle of exploratory speech, students exercise their innate drive to create and negotiate meaning. For students who have had little opportunity to do so, the process can be transforming.

That aspect of guided inquiry in science provides two additional benefits to students who face special challenges in learning, such as students with learning disabilities or minority students from inner-city areas, who often have difficulty using language to find meaning in abstract ideas. First, guided inquiry can make science content relevant to these students' own lives and, therefore, accessible to them. Second, it shows these students that language empowers them to find and unlock the meanings within ideas for themselves. In sharing knowledge (a key element in guided inquiry), a student must develop and articulate ideas and understandings more fully in order to express them, an important step in enhancing students' higher-order thinking skills.

The *National Science Education Standards* prescribes "the inclusion of all students in challenging science learning opportunities" and the "inclusion of those who traditionally have not received encouragement and opportunity to pursue science . . . students of color, students with disabilities, [and] students with limited English proficiency. . . . But all should have opportunities in the form of multiple experiences over several years" to master the principles and processes of science (National Research Council 1996).

The approaches that form the basis of guided inquiry are ideally suited to help all students achieve that goal.

Elementary Examples: Mirrors, My Sweet Tooth, and the Mystery Spill

As noted, elementary teachers tend more easily to integrate language learning with other subject areas. Because one teacher teaches all subjects, the teacher can use considerable imagination and discretion in using one subject area to highlight another.

In one simple instance, teacher David Keystone tells of his approach to using mirrors as the basis for melding science and literacy activities (Scott 1992). First, he asked children to talk about, then list, different things that can be done with mirrors. By writing and then comparing and contrasting lists, students grasp that language is the framework within which thoughts and knowledge are structured so that they can be retained and also communicated to others.

Then each child was given a pair of mirrors and some free time to experiment with them to discover their various uses. As they described their discoveries to classmates, the students gained practice in using language as the vehicle by which ideas are shared. Each student also kept a daily diary to answer a series of questions such as "What did I do?" and "What did I learn?" Keeping the diaries helped students understand that language can be the repository of facts, observations, ideas, and reflections—that language is the chief vehicle through which they express the scientific content they are learning. Expressing an idea through language helped the students give the idea a distinct identity and "shape," enabling them to integrate it into their personal understandings of the world.

Throughout the activity, the students listed questions that occurred to them: "How do you make a rainbow with a mirror?" and "Why are things backwards in mirrors?" Keystone asked his students to group their questions and reflections under three headings: "what I want to know or do," "how I will find out," and "what I will need." The lists strengthened students' sense that language can be used to differentiate between what they know and what they want to know and also to plan and predict.

Teachers can enhance these natural connections between science and literacy in elementary classrooms by applying the principles of guided inquiry. One such activity is My Sweet Tooth (SEPUP 1997), which helps students gather evidence and make decisions about the taste, nutritional value, and health implications of sugar and its substitutes.

Students begin the activity by brainstorming ideas about sweeteners in their diets. They might note that sugar is a source of energy and it makes sour foods taste better. One student might say, "Sugar makes you fat and gives you cavities, so our family uses artificial sweeteners"; another might respond, "Yuck! That stuff's made out of chemicals." The conversation helps students begin to define the properties of, and differences among, sweeteners.

Next, the activity leads students through three stages. In each, students use language in slightly different forms to gather information, evaluate it, and make evidence-based decisions. In the first stage, students note physical details; in the second, they record personal impressions; in the third, they read to fill gaps in their knowledge.

Working in small groups, students look closely at small samples of sugar and two artificial sweeteners. Students **note the details** of the materials' physical appearance, first by looking at them unaided and then by looking at the sweeteners through magnifiers. In discussions with their group members, students **compare and contrast** the magnified and unmagnified appearances of the various substances. Then the students make solutions of each of the three sweeteners, taste each one, and discuss and record their personal preferences along with the reasons behind their choices. (Note: Students with PKU, a genetic condition that makes them sensitive to aspartame, should not taste substances containing this artificial sweetener. Check with the school nurse to see if any students in your classroom suffer from PKU and also caution the class accordingly. In science, students usually are cautioned not to taste anything. In this or any other activity, students are allowed to taste only when instructed by the teacher.) The teacher asks students to choose which sweetener they would use at home and to explain to each other their reasons. The discussions help students use spoken language to explore and organize their knowledge and thoughts about sweeteners and to articulate them based on different kinds of evidence. Just as important, they use language to identify information they *do not* have but would need in order to make a better-informed choice.

At this point—when students are motivated to find out more—the teacher asks whether the students would like additional information before finalizing their decisions and, if so, what kinds of information they would like. Students are likely to know which sweetener tastes best to them, but perhaps the discussion has raised concerns, for example, "I like this one best, but is it good for me?" The teacher then distributes a page of background information about different sweeteners for students to read, asks them if their choices have changed, and then offers to help students conduct additional library or Internet research on sweeteners. Working through each stage, students come to learn that decisions can change as the evidence captured in language grows and changes.

To extend the activity's use of language, students can present their choices to classmates and explain their decisions. The presentations often initiate a discussion of the benefits and drawbacks of different kinds of sweeteners and why different people prefer different ones.

Throughout the activity, students are using many of the reciprocal processes that literacy and science share. Looking at the sweeteners, they **note physical details** and then **compare and contrast** the substances' appearances. They gain experience in understanding language operationally—experiencing a concept before learning its abstract name and definition, thereby being able to viscerally associate a term with a concrete meaning. They **infer,** from scientific studies using animals, how artificial sweeteners might affect humans. They **draw evidence-based conclusions** about which sweeteners they personally would or would not use. Through their observations and discussions, they use language to sort through evidence and to **distinguish facts from opinion.** As they read, write, discuss and debate, listen critically to other students, and work through a rudimentary scientific investigation, they also begin to understand that evidence can be a powerful factor in understanding the world.

My Sweet Tooth links science and language through the discussions as well as through students' answers to questions on the data sheets as they use evidence gained from reading and observation to explain and justify their decisions.

In addition, the activity's links between science and language can be broadened and strengthened through additional, student-designed investigations. For example, students could conduct a classroom-wide taste test between a regular cola and its low-calorie alternative, then graph the number of students who preferred the taste of each (or found no difference between them). Students also could write reports about the origins, benefits and drawbacks, and health implications of corn syrup, honey, cane sugar, and other sweeteners.

My Sweet Tooth also provides an effective way to sharpen students' response to media. The class can collect advertisements touting products that are "sugar-free," contain "no calories," or are made with "all-natural sugar." Students can dissect and compare the products' advertising strategies and even can write their own jingles or raps selling their preferred sweeteners.

Another guided inquiry for elementary students is called The Mystery Spill (SEPUP 1997). It deepens and extends the connection between classroom science experiences and social issues. The investigation introduces fifth and sixth graders to aspects of chemistry through a very real safety issue: the transport of hazardous wastes. The activity incorporates elements of a mystery, a game, and social action, all built on the twin cornerstones of science and literacy.

Before class begins or while students are out of the room, the teacher dumps some baking soda on a table or on the classroom floor. (To add a suggestion of realism, the teacher might overturn a toy truck beside the spilled material.) When students enter, the teacher announces that there has been a chemical spill in the classroom and that the students must determine what the spilled substance is and whether it is dangerous. The teacher discusses the meaning of the word *simulation* with students and explains that the material spilled here is not dangerous and that in a real emergency, anyone approaching a potentially hazardous material would wear safety goggles, gloves, and other protective gear. (Even so, beware of making the simulation too realistic. One teacher we know surrounded her spill in the school science lab with yellow "caution" tape. A colleague passing by in the hall saw the tape and the spill and notified the school office that there had been a chemical spill. The principal announced the spill over the school's public address system and told everyone to stay far away from the science lab.)

The students then discuss various ways to determine how the mystery substance might be tested. Does it burn? How does it react to water? They use language skills to **compare and contrast** different approaches, to **make inferences,** and to **predict** how different substances will react under different circumstances.

Each work group of four students is then given a small amount of six different substances that simulate hazardous materials. The first is labeled "corrosive," the second "flammable," the third "irritant," the fourth "oxidizer," the fifth "poison," and the sixth "radioactive." (In reality, the substances are citric acid, flour, detergent, baking soda, table salt, and sugar, respectively.) The students first **note the details** of each material's physical appearance and record their observations in a data table. Next, they test each material with moistened pH paper and note the color of the paper after the reaction. Finally, they add twenty drops of vinegar to each substance and observe the details of the reactions. The students describe all results in their data tables.

The teacher explains that the mystery substance is among one of the six kinds of materials the students have tested and that the students must now determine which category it belongs to. Each work group tests a small amount of the spilled powder with pH paper and then with vinegar. They **compare and contrast** the results with those listed in their data tables for the previous six materials tested, then **make inferences** and **draw conclusions** about the mystery spill's identity. The activity not only helps students understand that language is the repository of information but also shows them the importance of **sequencing events** within a process. Understanding the correct sequence of events is a necessary step in gathering information required to move from observation to **inference** and then to an ability to **draw conclusions.**

Another aspect of the activity can help students **link words with precise meanings.** The teacher hangs a poster showing the colors and wording of eight diamond-shaped placards. Each placard represented shows the word for the kind of material inside—"radioactive" or "infectious substance," for example—and the distinctive logo that represents that category of hazard. The poster launches a discussion of the practical meaning of scientific terms such as *flammable* and *oxidizer.*

The teacher then distributes worksheets divided into eight squares, with each square containing the design of a placard warning of a specific hazard. The students color the designs and cut them out. On the same sheet there are eight additional squares that the students cut out. Each square contains the definition of a term listed on the placards. The students then play a matching game, linking the definition printed on a square with the appropriate colored square representing the hazardous material.

The Mystery Spill activity can lead students to create their own investigations that also join the skills of science and literacy while helping students understand the meaning of the activity in their own lives. For example, perhaps trucks with diamond-shaped placards pass the school. Students might decide that there are just too many trucks carrying hazardous materials past the school. Some students might think that the trucks should be banned from traveling through town. Other students may have parents who work at a factory that uses those hazardous materials and fear that their mothers or fathers will lose their jobs if such a ban is implemented. The resulting debate could lead to additional research: What is the likelihood that there will be a spill? How many people would be affected? What could the damage be?

The students then can use language skills to present the scientific evidence they have collected to support their opinions. Some might write letters to the editor of the local paper presenting evidence to **predict** the odds of an eventual spill; others may write newspaper editorials **comparing and contrasting** the odds of a spill with the possible economic consequences for the town of banning the trucks. They might arrange a mock debate before a "city council" of their peers or parents and undertake a science project to design spill-proof containers for hazardous materials.

Throughout the activity, students constantly employ the processes of literacy to sharpen and illuminate their understanding of scientific facts, concepts, and processes. At the same time, they use their newly gained scientific knowledge to shape their use of language in articulating evidence-based choices and decisions and making their cases to others.

When students can relate activities to issues in their own lives and communities, they develop a visceral understanding of the interdependent roles of science and language in developing and using evidence to reach decisions about societal issues.

A Middle School Example: The Fruitvale Story

This investigation (SEPUP 2002) is centered around a practical problem that puts the student in the central role of investigator and decision maker. Students are asked to imagine that they are college students coming home to the town of Fruitvale for summer vacation. While there, they become embroiled in a local investigation of polluted water. (We now describe the activity in the second person, both for simplicity's sake and so that readers may more easily put themselves in the student's place.)

When you arrive home, hot and thirsty from the long bus ride, you go to the kitchen sink for a drink of cold water. Your mother tells you not to drink the water—that, for the last few months, water in the creek behind the house has had a funny smell. The family members now only drink bottled water because they fear that their well might be contaminated.

You begin to investigate. Your family and the one next door are the only families in the area still drawing water from their own wells; everyone else uses city water. The neighbors still drink from their own well, but they mention that their dog has been sick and wonder if he might have drunk bad water from the creek. You also learn that water wells drilled beneath a new housing development nearby, next to a farm, have been found to be contaminated with pesticide.

You begin to keep a journal. In it, you record the facts you find, your questions and conjectures, and your conclusions, inferences, and predictions about the meaning of the evidence you compile. You also make a map of the area to place important sites in relation to one another. You note additional pieces of evidence you must gather to determine the source of the water's funny smell. You write down a sequenced series of steps you could take to collect that evidence. You conclude which three sites around Fruitvale are the most likely sources of the pollution and explain in your journal the reasons and evidence that led you to predict those sources.

Next, you talk with workers at the city water department. You learn that the pesticide has been found at five times its maximum safe level in one well on the housing development. The pesticide manufacturer, whose factory is also adjacent to the farm, originally had thought that the chemical would safely decompose in every kind of soil. That was not the case and the compound was banned in the United States eight years ago. City officials fear that old residues of the pesticide may be leaching into Fruitvale's main water wells.

The city has enough money in the budget to drill twelve test wells to map the spread of the pesticide beneath Fruitvale's soil. Impressed with your methodical investigation, the city water department manager asks you to help select the combination of test sites that will yield the most accurate and complete information.

Now students go to work in the classroom. In the first activity, students examine the concepts of porosity and permeability to understand the properties of an aquifer and an aquitard.

The teacher asks students to predict how long water will take to move through various earth materials, such as soil, clay, sand, and gravel. Students are asked to rank the materials according to the speed with which the students think water will pass through them. After students record their predictions, the teacher pours 30 to 35 ml of water through each material in turn. Students record the amount of water poured in, measure the time the water takes to move through each material and drain into a container underneath, and also measure the quantities of water that exit the material. (The teacher points out that the results from one material may lead students to alter their predictions for others.) Students record the results in their journals.

The activity engages students directly in scientific processes: it asks students to begin with a hypothesis, take quantitative measurements, tabulate data, and compare the results with their predictions, just as conventional science experiments do. The activity also enlists the reciprocal skills of science and literacy as they **note details** (the exact amount of time water takes to move through a material), **compare and contrast** the transmission times of the various materials, and use evidence to **separate fact from opinion** about how long the water will take to move—and, of course, to write these details clearly and concisely in their journals.

As the inquiry unfolds, the journal becomes a crucial tool in linking literacy and science. It serves as a record not only of the evidence they gather, but also of their questions and speculations about what the evidence means and how individual facts relate to one another. The journal enables a student to erect a personal scaffold of language on which to assemble data, observations, and other evidence. It also provides a repository for speculations, reflections, and questions awaiting additional data for answers. The journal becomes a reflective space in which students use language to knit together their scientific data and evidence, their ideas, and their inferences and conclusions. It is in their journals where students are constantly asking themselves, "What new insights do I have that I didn't have before? What do these new insights mean for Fruitvale's water quality? What don't I know and how will I find out?"

A journal becomes both a tool for, and a record of, each student's personal growth in scientific understanding and skill. Therefore, it also can serve as an assessment tool. By comparing a student's writing in a journal against a list of performance expectations for journal writing, the teacher can gauge the student's growth in science and in written language. To keep students focused as they write, teachers can give them the same list of performance expectations, which students often paste inside the front covers of their journals for reference. (The next five chapters provide teachers with detailed literacy performance expectations that they can use in science activities to help students improve language skills over time. The chapters also show how these expectations can be applied as assessment tools if teachers choose to do so.)

Next, to understand the degree of risk lurking in Fruitvale's tainted water, students need to grasp the concepts of "parts per million" and "parts per billion." Working in groups, students use cups and eyedroppers to create progressively weaker solutions of colored water. Students must carefully observe and record the presence, absence, and strength of color in each cup. As they do, they develop skills in observing and collecting quantitative data. They then use language to interpret their observations and to explore, clarify, and express their thinking about the presence of the pollutant in the solution. As they record their data in their journals, they **note details, sequence events,** and **make inferences** and **draw conclusions** about why groups' results differ, leading to a discussion about human error, variability in the test samples, and so on.

As students use those skills of science, they also are strengthening the reciprocal skills of literacy as they use written language to **note details, record the sequence of events, compare and contrast** possible explanations and courses of action as they grapple to **link cause and effect,** and reflect on what they are learning. As students work in groups to gather and analyze data, plan, and interpret results, they also practice the same literacy skills verbally and aurally that their journals strengthen through writing.

After reading the details of the story, students are ready to test Fruitvale's water. They are presented with a map of forty possible well sites around the town and are asked to use information from the story, and clues from previous activities recorded in their journals, to decide where to drill twelve test wells. In other words, they must use the scientific concepts and skills they have gained through the activities in conjunction with fundamental literacy skills: they must **note details** from the story, **compare and contrast** various drilling schemes, and **make inferences and draw conclusions** about which plan will yield the most useful information. Formulating a plan and describing it in detail in their journals also give students experience in weighing alternatives and making trade-offs, key skills in science and in making satisfying choices in one's personal life.

Again working in groups of three or four, students then "test the wells": they draw water from sample bottles that have been formulated with different concentrations of pH buffers, then add one or two drops of a universal indicator. Students assign each well a numerical rank of 0 through 5, depending on the parts per billion of pesticide each contains as judged by the color of each water sample after the reaction. After testing a group of three wells and tabulating the data in their journals, students review and perhaps revise their drilling plans, then test another three wells. As they review and revise, the students **note details** of their results and use them to **compare and contrast** possible alternatives, then to **make predictions** about which sites would be most informative to drill next.

When all test results are in, each group of students maps the area of Fruitvale that seems to have groundwater unsafe for humans to ingest (defined as test wells with a contamination of 1 or higher). The teacher asks students why the map needs to be as accurate as possible. The ensuing discussion about determining risk, plotting the movement of contaminants, and cleanup procedures emphasizes the importance of **noting detail, comparing and contrasting** well readings and alternative plans, **making inferences,** and ultimately **drawing conclusions** to arrive at a workable plan.

Next, the groups **compare and contrast** their maps and talk about the reasons for similarities and differences. They also weigh the value of the information that would be gained by drilling additional test wells against the expense and time it would take to gain the extra information. This step requires students to demonstrate an operational understanding of science vocabulary— first in their individual journals to sort out and order their own ideas, then in discussions to communicate, compare, and contrast their findings and opinions (another essential step in science).

This discussion leads to a final activity, one that knits together the skills and processes of science and literacy even more tightly. In a town meeting, students take on roles representing Fruitvale's residents, parents, public officials such as the mayor or the manager of the city water system, executives of the local chemical company, and pollution cleanup experts. The student-actors and audience use the evidence compiled in their journals and knowledge gained from the activities to debate the merits of various approaches to, and plans for, cleaning up the contamination.

In this culminating activity, students must marshal the facts and processes of science that they have learned in previous facets of the investigation, interrelate ideas, and integrate their ideas and information. At the same time, they also must rely on the skills of literacy to discuss together, and reach consensus about, what the science has told them. They must fuse their knowledge of scientific facts and processes with the skills of language to reason through evidence to make an informed decision—and to express their views, listen effectively, counter opposing arguments, and persuade others. They must **note the details** of the well tests and of what others say, **distinguishing fact from opinion.** They must **sequence events** to determine the source of the contamination and to **link cause and effect,** both in analyzing the test results and in making an effective argument. They must **compare and contrast** the positions taken by themselves and others to understand how they differ and how they complement one another. Finally, they must **make inferences** and **draw conclusions** in order to **make predictions** about the relative effectiveness of competing cleanup schemes.

An activity such as Fruitvalue draws together all aspects of literacy—reading, writing, listening, speaking, and analyzing media—in the service of good science. In addition, the activity helps students construct their own internal processes of collecting, ordering, and employing evidence to reach personal decisions.

As students work, teachers can monitor students' growth in literacy by comparing their use of language against several sets of explicit performance expectations, then tracking their progress using running records (see Chapter 6) or rubrics.

For example, teachers can observe students in learning groups and in mock debates to gauge each student's skills in group interaction, such as whether the student listens carefully or responds appropriately to questions. Teachers also can compare students' drafts of narrative procedures against a list of performance expectations. Does the student use the right words to express intended meanings? Does the student sequence events accurately as well as clearly enough for others to follow? In writing a narrative procedure to enable another person to reproduce the investigation and result, the student learns the power of words (and precision in using them) to shape actions and determine their outcomes.

The skills and procedures students learn in the Fruitvale activity translate directly to environmental issues beyond the classroom, giving students ample opportunities to employ their new knowledge in their own lives and communities in order to develop an "enduring understanding" (Wiggins and McTighe 1998).

A High School Example: Using Evidence to Weigh Alternatives

Students are presented with a scenario: to stimulate business investment and promote its emerging market economy, the Chinese government is opening land controlled by the state to private development. Its latest offering is two hundred acres on the outskirts of Beijing (SEPUP 2000).

Students examine satellite photos of the region taken several years apart to learn the patterns and features of surrounding development. Then the students divide into eight interest groups, each promoting a distinctly different use for the land: a residential area, a car factory, a park and nature preserve, a nuclear power plant, farmland, a water reservoir, a wastewater treatment plant, and an amusement park. Each group must make as compelling a presentation as possible for its point of view before the Beijing land-use committee—including a plan to remediate any harmful environmental effects of the proposed use. The groups must gather and organize data, prepare to answer the committee's probing questions, and be ready to rebut negative evidence and comments about their positions that competing groups put forward, all while remaining within the strict time limit that the committee has allowed for each presentation.

Each group must research and gather as much data and information as possible relevant to its position—the economic and environmental impacts of its proposal, the plan's costs and returns, its benefits and drawbacks. (Usually, the research and presentation assignments are parceled out so that one student researches and prepares a single aspect of the group's presentation.)

The activity calls on high school students to integrate their skills of scientific research and data organization with their skills in language, and to stretch both to new limits. To make their cases, the students must **note the scientific details** that favor or weaken their positions. They must use evidence to **make inferences** and **draw conclusions** about the advantages and disadvantages of their plan for the land. Those steps, in turn, require them to **predict** from evidence the positive and negative outcomes of the land use they urge, which means that they must **link cause and effect** and **distinguish fact from opinion.** Finally, they must **compare and contrast** the strong and weak points of their case with others so that they can argue more forcefully for their views.

In making their presentations, they must rely on the power of their language to present their evidence as strongly as they can. They must **note the details** of opposing arguments and **compare and contrast** those arguments, both with their own ideas and with the evidence that they have gathered. They must be ready to **predict** any negative consequences of opposing land uses that those groups try to conceal, **linking cause and effect** and **distinguishing fact from opinion** as they do so. (Part of that process involves **linking words and meanings** so students can internalize those meanings and make those words part of their repertoire—in this example, to make sure that opposing groups are not using deceptive language.) Throughout the presentations, the students will exercise their analytical skills, asking questions such as, "What is the source of this information?" and "What evidence is *not* being presented?" (Once developed, these skills can be applied just as effectively to television commercials, political ideologies, and other messages intended to persuade.)

Students can apply the skills and insights they have gained from the activity to conduct similar comparisons, debates, and investigations of their own designs about issues in their own communities.

Conclusion: Blending Language and Inquiry in Science Education

Inquiry-based activities that address issues personal to students are more than engrossing. Data shows that students who work through guided inquiries such as My Sweet Tooth, the Fruitvale activity, and the Beijing land-use debate understand science concepts at least as well as students who are taught through textbooks, lectures, and worksheets. Teachers who regularly use guided-inquiry science materials in their classrooms report that students understand science concepts more deeply and thoroughly than students who learn through more traditional methods.

But guided inquiry brings an additional advantage: it enlists language as a key element in the development of students' scientific knowledge and skills, giving teachers a powerful additional resource to help more students achieve high standards. Guided inquiry recognizes that language and its skills are the lenses that focus students' thinking, the catalysts that help students turn facts into knowledge that they can retain long past their school careers and apply in their own lives.

3

Tools for the New Science Literacy
Performance Expectations, Student Metacognition Strategies, and Strategies for Explicit Teaching

A true journey of discovery lies not in seeking new shores but in finding new eyes.

—MARCEL PROUST

Successfully implementing the new science literacy in any classroom depends on the synergy created by combining three interconnected approaches: specific performance expectations for students, strategies for explicit teaching, and student metacognition techniques.

When performance standards are explicit, students know *what* improvement looks like. Teachers use strategies for explicit teaching to show students *how* to improve. Students then can use metacognitive techniques to continue to progress *on their own*, without teachers' repeated intervention. In short, the three-part approach enables students to become independent and, therefore, lifelong learners.

Performance Expectations

To know whether they are improving in their science-related use of language, students need clear, easy-to-follow guidelines that point them toward improvement. At the same time, teachers need easy-to-use tools to determine whether students are improving their language skills in ways that enhance science learning.

As an initial toolkit, we offer what we have termed *performance expectations*. The brief lists of expectations serve as short reminders that can focus the attention of students and teachers on key skills of literacy that necessarily are called upon in the course of good science teaching and learning.

The expectations' purpose is to give students and teachers a single, shared list of criteria for good performance in literacy skills while doing and learning science, a goal implied throughout the *National Science Education Standards*. The standards declare that "students must become familiar with ... rules of evidence, ways of formulating questions, and ways of proposing explanations" (National Research Council 1996). The standards also define scientific literacy as not only "knowledge and understanding of science subject matter" but also "understanding [of] the nature of science, the scientific enterprise, and the role of science in society and personal life." Teachers and students cannot achieve these goals set by the standards without acknowledging and using the intimate connection between science content and the skilled use of language.

The performance expectations are designed for both students and teachers to use. Teachers can use the expectations to monitor students' progress over time. Students can use them, with the teacher's help, as road maps to independent learning and greater skill. When both students and teachers measure students' work against the same explicit performance expectations targeted to grade level, both can closely track students' growth in achieving literacy goals within the science program.

The groups of performance expectations presented here have evolved through my work with teachers at all grade levels, helping them incorporate the tools and techniques of literacy into their science programs. As a foundation, I have used the literacy standards established by the New Standards project, a joint initiative of the Learning Research and Development Center at the University of Pittsburgh and the National Center for Education and the Economy. I then connected those literacy goals and ideas to the goals embodied in the National Science Education Standards.

The result is a framework of performance expectations that have proven, through teachers' use and experience in working classrooms, to be effective. However, educators easily might find ways to refine, adjust, or customize them to specific projects in ways that heighten the expectations' power to guide and track students' progress. In that sense, all of the performance expectations listed here can be viewed as generic—templates or suggestions that individual educators can shape and adjust to fit their own classroom needs and programs.

We have included specific, detailed lists of performance expectations for reading, writing, speaking, listening, and media analysis. To give teachers practical examples, we show how relevant groups of expectations might be used in the guided-inquiry activities described in the following chapters.

We also have included performance expectations and teaching and meta-cognition strategies in two related areas: group interaction and persuasive strategies. We have added those two areas because both increasingly are crucial skills in political and social policy discussions as well as in the workplace. For example, science and engineering are deeply technical but also highly collaborative: a researcher, and particularly an engineer, rarely works alone on a technical project. The larger the project is, the more communication among diverse individuals there must be. When Boeing designed its 777 passenger jet, for example, it formed 238 separate design teams. The typical team included specialized Boeing engineers, aircraft maintenance workers, and representatives of Boeing's suppliers, shippers, and passenger groups, each imposing their own demands and constraints on the design. If such a project is to be completed efficiently, communication among such disparate groups must be as thorough, concise, and error-free as possible. That result depends on the ability of those involved to use the learned skills of speaking, listening, and other forms of negotiating through language that frame interaction.

Outside of technical fields, group dynamics and information transactions also play an increasingly central role in determining an individual's success in life and work. If a problem is to be solved, the person defining the problem and recommending a particular solution—parent, politician, or corporate executive—must use evidence to make a persuasive case. Therefore, knowing how to work smoothly with others to marshal evidence, evaluate information, and make decisions is a skill that has been raised to the same plane of importance as reading, writing, listening, and speaking. The guided inquiry-based science classroom provides students with countless opportunities to work in groups, and the related performance expectations offered here can help students and their teachers gain the most from those opportunities.

How students benefit

Performance expectations are to be shared with students. When presented effectively by the teacher, the expectations show students not only the goals that they are expected to achieve but also what they need to do in their work to achieve those goals. When used effectively, performance expectations can empower students in three ways.

First, students can use each group of performance expectations as a set of explicit personal strategies to guide and improve their work. Too often, when a teacher tells a student that the student needs to "do better," the student is left wondering what "better" looks like. Learners who struggle without success often feel paralyzed; they don't know what good learners do in order to succeed. When teachers share performance expectations with students, teachers let students in on the strategies that good learners employ intuitively. With these performance expectations in hand, students then can know more clearly what is expected of them. They have a clear path to follow in improving their own work instead of waiting for a teacher to render judgment. When they know and understand explicit performance expectations, students are empowered to take charge of their own learning and improvement, which also lifts some instructional burden from the teacher.

Second, when used as guidelines for achievement, the expectations help shift a student's motivation and sense of control from an external source—the teacher or a grade—to an internal one: their desire to succeed.

Third, the expectations demystify reading and writing. They help students understand the specific steps they can take to become better readers. The expectations also help students understand that, in practical terms, writing can be thought of as "just talking that's been written down"—and, therefore, as something that they are capable of doing.

When first confronting a set of performance expectations, students may not be able to use them without help. Even middle and high school students may not clearly understand what it means to "exclude extraneous details" from a lab report or to "compare and contrast" the arguments in two essays expressing different views on the safety of genetically modified foods, for example. The teacher needs to invest adequate time to demonstrate to students how to use the expectations to guide them as they read or write, or prepare or critique a class presentation.

Once they understand how to use the expectations as self-improvement tools, students gain the knowledge and independence they need to begin to help themselves use language more effectively as they do science.

As noted earlier, I am keenly aware of the pressures on class time. However, from extensive practical experience, I can assure the reader that time invested effectively here will reap rich dividends as the school year progresses.

How teachers benefit

The performance expectations are designed to empower not only students but also teachers at all grade levels.

For example, many elementary teachers are less certain of their own command of science content than they are of their ability to teach language skills and, therefore, lack confidence in their ability to teach science effectively (Abell and Roth 1992; Tobin and Holman 1992). For those teachers, the performance expectations can help highlight the links and the common territory between the two disciplines, such as identifying logical fallacies or using evidence to justify a statement. Teachers can use the literacy techniques they are comfortable with to broaden their teaching programs to less familiar areas. The performance expectations presented here can help those teachers identify key language skills to cultivate in their students and then link those skills to the content-rich context of children's boundless curiosity about the natural world.

For middle and high school teachers, the performance expectations fulfill a different function. These teachers are science specialists. They cannot be expected to understand in depth the techniques of teaching reading or helping students become better readers of content information. In addition, these teachers typically are not used to the idea that they can help students grow in literacy skills over time.

The good news is that science teachers need not become English teachers. Instead, these performance expectations can help science teachers support literacy as a key element of their science programs. By identifying and exploiting the endless opportunities that science offers to use language clearly and precisely, science teachers can foster the growth of those skills in their students—and, as a result, teach science more effectively.

Not an assessment or grading scheme

We have dubbed these checkpoints "performance expectations" in a deliberate attempt to differentiate them from any kind of formal assessment or grading protocols. Establishing assessment systems is the purview of teachers and administrators. Just as important, teachers need not alter or abandon their existing assessment systems or practices to effectively adopt and use these performance expectations.

Educators can use these performance expectations as loosely or as formally as they choose. Some teachers might use them only as rough yardsticks for spot-checking the work of underachievers; others might choose to organize each set of performance expectations as a rubric to track each student's progress in one or more areas throughout the school year. The expectations are flexible enough to let an individual teacher do either or to create her own expectations to fulfill a specific need in a particular classroom activity.

All performance expectations are listed in the Appendix for teachers to photocopy for their own use as well as to distribute to students.

A fundamental performance expectation. One performance expectation underlies all others, regardless of their origins. Any time that a student uses language, **the student should be expected to demonstrate a proper command of the language appropriate to the student's developmental level.** Consequently, performance expectations for general use of the language are an inseparable part of all other expectations for students' language activities. That overarching expectation requires that the student demonstrates an understanding of proper usage, the conventions of language, and the rules of grammar (appropriate to grade level) in all forms of writing and speaking, including such elements as

- proper verb tenses and forms;
- proper vocabulary;
- sentence construction;
- paragraph construction;
- punctuation; and
- spelling.

Some teachers or entire schools establish style guides that students and teachers can use as a common reference to determine what is proper in punctuation, grammar, and usage. If no such guide is readily available, science teachers may wish to ask their schools' or districts' language department for guidance or for help in compiling guides appropriate to grade levels.

Student Metacognition Strategies

Metacognitive strategies are explicitly designed to help students become aware of their own thought processes and to modify them to make those processes more effective. When students recognize their patterns of thinking, they also can become aware of the signals that tell them that they are having difficulty comprehending or expressing. However, many students cannot become better at using and processing language unless teachers help them cultivate the metacognitive skills of reflection and analysis. When students understand explicitly what good readers do to improve their comprehension, students understand how to help themselves when they encounter difficulties. By guiding students to that understanding, teachers can lead students to adopt specific strategies that they can use to learn and improve on their own. These strategies enable students to build their capacity to learn independently, without the teacher's continuing demonstrations or intervention.

A report by the National Research Council's Committee on Learning Research and Educational Practice underscores the point. "Because metacognition often takes the form of an internal conversation, it can easily be assumed that individuals will develop the internal dialogue on their own"—the assumption underlying implicit teaching (Donovan, Bransford, and Pellegrino 1999). However, "because metacognition often takes the form of an internal dialogue, many students may be unaware of its importance unless the processes are explicitly emphasized by teachers. . . . Research has demonstrated that children can be taught these strategies, including the ability to predict outcomes, explain to oneself in order to improve understanding, note failures to comprehend, [and] plan ahead."

The report also emphasizes the importance of teaching metacognitive skills explicitly. "Each of these techniques shares a strategy of teaching and modeling the process . . . class discussions are used to support skill development, with the goal of independence and self-regulation."

Explicit metacognitive teaching strategies work, the report states. "Evidence from research indicates that when these . . . principles are incorporated into teaching, student achievement improves. Teaching metacognitive strategies in context has been shown to improve understanding in physics, written composition, and . . . mathematical problem solving." The study emphasizes the idea that teaching language skills and science in the context of each other can further leverage the power of explicit metacognitive strategies.

"Integration of metacognitive instruction with discipline-based learning can . . . help students learn to take control of their own learning by defining learning goals and monitoring their progress in achieving them," the report concludes.

The student metacognition techniques detailed in the following chapters are included as concise lists in the Appendix, ready for teachers to photocopy and distribute to students to use in guiding their own ongoing improvement.

Strategies for Explicit Teaching

Merging literacy and science does not mean that teachers now must teach two distinctly different subjects within the same limitations of time and other resources in which they used to teach one.

When choosing teaching strategies that combine the two disciplines, teachers can find approaches that show students how they can help themselves learn and improve. To that end, the strategies explored in the next four chapters are **explicit** rather than implicit.

The language teaching strategies employed in science classrooms are too often implicit: teachers assume that if a student reads a book, fills out a data sheet, or writes a report, the student's language skills will somehow automatically improve. But teachers know from long experience, as well as from test scores, that this is not the case.

Effective language teaching within the context of science is explicit teaching: the teacher chooses a specific learning strategy, explains and demonstrates it explicitly to students, then guides and coaches them as they adopt the strategy as a tool to help them learn science more effectively. Explicit teaching helps students cultivate skills that enable them to become independent, lifelong learners.

The teaching strategies described here offer a few examples of ways in which teachers can "teach for independence"; many of the strategies shift the locus of effort and control from the teacher to the student. When used effectively, such strategies can free the teacher from a good deal of repetitive instruction. With that freedom, the teacher can use a greater range of professional skills to lead students to higher levels of achievement and satisfaction—in mastering science concepts as well as in using language to articulate them.

In other words, fusing the two disciplines within the context of guided inquiry-based science actually can make the teacher's job easier and richer, not harder. It can do so for four reasons.

First, the ability to use and understand language effectively is essential to good science. Skill with language and skill in science cannot be separated. The better students are able to draw meaning from—and infuse meaning into—language, the better science students they will be.

Second, the language skills emphasized and strengthened during guided inquiry-based science activities are embedded in the activities themselves. Students need to use the skills in order to do science. These are not language techniques that teachers need to drill students on or hand out worksheets for. Teachers demonstrate the skills; students adopt them and use them as templates of effective habits for doing better science.

Third, the more effectively students are able to use language, the easier and more satisfying the teacher's work can become: students who have a greater facility with language are more easily able to understand, discuss, and apply scientific concepts and processes. When students are able to use language skillfully enough to clearly communicate their ideas, teachers can better understand their learning patterns and styles and, ultimately, whether each student is actually learning. Teachers can more precisely understand what students are thinking and no longer have to wonder whether fuzzy ideas are a product of poor facility with language or of fuzzy thinking.

Fourth, therefore, the effort and time that teachers give to strengthening students' language skills through science is an investment, not an expense. The work the teacher expends can pay practical dividends far greater than the effort. A relatively small amount of time spent imparting literacy skills to science students will save the teacher even more time later—time that the teacher then can use to lead students to higher levels of understanding than otherwise might be possible.

Most of the strategies include outlines for teachers and lists of performance guidelines that should be given to students. The guidelines, checklists, and graphic organizers discussed also are included in the Appendix, ready for photocopying.

How the Teaching and Learning Strategies Are Organized

We have provided a separate chapter for each of the specific literacy skills of reading, writing, speaking and listening, and media literacy and analysis, the last of which weaves together skills from the other literacy areas. Each chapter offers several instructional approaches to that area of literacy. For each approach, the chapter lists relevant performance expectations, describes explicit teaching strategies, and suggests student metacognitive techniques. We also have shown how many of the approaches might be used in the classroom activities described in Chapter 2.

These lists and suggestions are not intended to be recipes or prescriptions. They are intended not only for teachers to try and adapt but also as starting points or inspirations that teachers can use to create their own strategies, expectations, and metacognition techniques.

Conclusion: The Synergy of a Threefold Approach

Performance expectations in each area of literacy directly support students' science learning. The expectations help students understand how to more effectively express the scientific concepts, facts, and skills they are mastering. As a result, the expectations also allow teachers to gauge students' progress not only in language but also in science: If a student is unable to express an idea clearly, how will the teacher know if the student actually understands it? In other words, is the student's problem a deficiency in understanding the content or one in expressing that understanding? Teasing the two problems apart can be even more frustrating for the teacher than the student; "I know it but I can't explain it" is not an adequate foundation for accurate assessment. Incorporating literacy and its performance expectations into science education often can resolve the dilemma. If students gain new skills in expression, they will be able to recognize for themselves weaknesses in their conceptual understanding.

Just as important, the expectations enable teachers to track students' improvements in science and language skills without needing to learn elaborate new assessment schemes or devote significantly more time to assessing students' work.

Teaching strategies that successfully combine science and literacy are based on three principles.

First, guided inquiry-based science in the classroom naturally presents countless opportunities to improve students' science learning by strengthening their abilities to use language. Teachers need not replace their current inquiry-based curriculum or their teaching methods or styles to blend the two disciplines. Rather, teachers need only to be aware of opportunities to emphasize students' attention to, and care with, language in the course of science inquiry.

Second, effective teaching strategies for uniting science and language are metacognitive. The strategies demand from students a sophisticated use of language as a primary tool with which to explore their science experiences and the meanings of those experiences in their own lives. The metacognitive skills and techniques that students develop through these activities help them "learn how to learn."

Third, by investing a manageable amount of effort and imagination, a teacher can expand almost any science inquiry to embrace language skills more deliberately and completely. That bit of extra effort is not a cost, but an investment that is repaid in students' greater mastery of science as well as language.

The combination of performance expectations and strategies for explicit teaching enables students to make effective use of **metacognitive techniques** to guide their own work and improve on their own, freeing them from an orientation to grades or teachers' judgments. With proper modeling and coaching by the teacher, the techniques can become part of students' habits of mind and empower them to become lifelong learners. They begin to understand the power of self-assessment as a tool for taking charge of their own learning.

The primary task of any educator who teaches science is to help students master science concepts and processes. The secondary task is to help students improve their language skills within the context of science. Performance expectations, strategies for explicit teaching, and students' metacognitive techniques form the structure of support that teachers and students can use to reach both goals simultaneously.

4

Reading
Paths to Better Comprehension

Most of the fundamental ideas of science are essentially simple and may, as a rule, be expressed in a language comprehensible to everyone.
—ALBERT EINSTEIN

Educators who teach science are concerned mainly with students' ability to read and understand science content as a way to integrate science concepts into their subjective understanding of the world. Therefore, these performance expectations and teaching and learning strategies for reading target the crucial issue of comprehension.

In all but the lowest grades, most students (except some of those from deprived backgrounds or those for whom English is a second language) understand the mechanics of reading and can decode print reasonably well. Research shows that in middle school, for example, comprehending what is read, not decoding it, gives students the most trouble. (Teachers who suspect that a student is unable to properly decode words should consult with the language department to ensure that the student's problem is accurately diagnosed and addressed outside of the science classroom.)

However, the conventional "teaching strategy" too often chosen to address *all* reading problems is to send large numbers of these students to remedial classes that, more often than not, dwell on the mechanics of decoding. The only thing students gain is an even greater sense that reading, and therefore learning, is an incomprehensible process. As Schoenbach et al. note, "For such students, being sent back to the beginning of reading instruction only reinforces their misconception that reading is just saying words" (1999).

In guided inquiry-based science activities, teachers can use the techniques of inquiry itself to help students improve their understanding of what they read. More important, teachers can combine those techniques with the principles of metacognition to equip students with intellectual tools that they can use on their own—eventually without prompting—to become better readers and, therefore, better learners.

The teaching and learning strategies for comprehension in this chapter all are designed to help students learn to

- understand the purpose of reading a specific text;
- effectively preview the material to improve comprehension while reading;
- monitor their understanding of the reading to make sure that they are grasping its meaning;
- extract correct meaning even when they encounter difficulties; and
- identify and be able to summarize a reading's main and subordinate ideas.

If students can accomplish these goals, they not only will comprehend what they read but also will develop strategies that will enable them to become self-supporting learners.

Performance Expectations for Reading Comprehension

These performance expectations (p. 147) help students learn how to comprehend what they read. The expectations also help teachers discover whether students actually did comprehend. Through explicit teaching, teachers can impart the expectations to students in the form of self-help strategies that students then can apply in activities. By using the metacognitive techniques in inquiry-based activities, students learn to use the techniques on their own to improve their work. If they choose to, teachers can use the same criteria in assessing students' performance and improvement.

Performance expectations for reading comprehension. The student:

- **Makes accurate interpretations, inferences, conclusions, and real-world connections about the text.** Students can explain in their own words the themes and main points of what has been read and find relevant passages in the text to support their assertions.
- **Supports personal understandings and interpretations of the text with detail and convincing evidence.** Students can find relevant

passages in the reading that not only support their assertions but also convince others that the assertions are correct.

- **Uses evidence to interpret and apply ideas.** Students can see personal meanings in the reading and apply those meanings outside of the classroom.

- **Compares and contrasts themes and ideas**. Students can identify related themes or topics in different passages or texts and explain their similarities and differences. For example, in making an evidence-based personal decision about which sweetener to use, students compare and contrast facts gleaned from their readings.

- **Makes perceptive and well-developed connections among concepts in the reading** (even if the author does not make them explicitly) and between ideas in the reading and the student's own life.

- **Identifies and evaluates writing strategies to understand how the author presents a point of view.** Students are able to identify the author's assumptions, biases, and intent and critically analyze the effectiveness of the author's message.

To see how students might actually use these expectations to guide their work in an activity, we can return to My Sweet Tooth, described in Chapter 2.

In the activity, students gather information about sugar and artificial sweeteners, then make evidence-based decisions about which to use. As part of the activity, they read product labels and information about sugar substitutes. Students can demonstrate their comprehension of the material they read by using facts presented in the reading as evidence in ongoing discussions in their work groups about the merits and drawbacks of each substance. That allows them to **make and support warranted assertions** from the text and to **use evidence from their reading to support their assertions**. By using the evidence to justify their personal decisions, students demonstrate their ability to **use evidence to interpret and apply ideas** to their own lives.

As part of My Sweet Tooth, teachers often encourage students to search the library or the Internet for more information about sweeteners. Usually, students find an array of articles and studies with sometimes conflicting messages. To interpret the materials' collective meanings as accurately as possible, the students must **evaluate the information and presentation strategies** of the materials' authors. Was a study declaring a sweetener to be safe for humans paid for or written by the company that makes it? Does the study include negative information about the sweetener's effects on people that a previous report found? If so, how prominently in the study is that negative information featured? What strategies does the writer of the study use to confront (or dismiss) that negative information? This kind of analysis joins conventional reading comprehension—understanding the meaning expressed through the words—to the comprehension of an author's intention and purpose called for by the techniques of media analysis.

Student Metacognition Strategies for Reading Comprehension

The performance expectations for reading comprehension are embodied in a series of metacognitive strategies that teachers can share with students. The strategies help students become aware of their own thought patterns, habits, and processes. Once aware, students can use the strategies as practical tools to help themselves exchange less effective habits and patterns for more effective ones, the ones that good readers use intuitively. Mastering those new thought processes enables students to reflect upon what they have read, a key skill if students are to become independent seekers of knowledge.

Teachers can impart these metacognitive strategies to students through a variety of strategies for explicit teaching. When students are able to use a set of metacognitive tools for reading content material (in contrast to reading for the sake of learning to read), they read more purposefully and, therefore, with more understanding (Donovan, Bransford, and Pellegrino 1999; Schoenbach et al. 1999). When used effectively, metacognitive reading strategies resemble "a storyteller in your head," as one student put it: "When you read," she explained, "there should be a little voice in your head, like a storyteller is saying it. If that's not there, then you're just looking at the words" (Schoenbach et al. 1999).

Students must use these kinds of strategies to achieve comprehension performance expectations when they take part in Chapter 2's activity in which they debate the use of an open plot of land in Beijing. In the activity, students divide into groups, with each advocating one of eight possible uses for the tract. To be effective, the students must read for evidence to evaluate the impact of their recommended use for the land as well as that of competing plans.

Students can organize and streamline their research efforts by **predicting** from titles and other summary or introductory information what particular pieces of material can tell them. They can determine **what the reading is likely to be about** and **what they are likely to learn from it.** By asking themselves what they already know about the topic, they can **monitor and adjust their reading strategies to better identify relevant themes and passages in the text.** Such passages can help them **identify aspects of the topic that they still want to know about or still do not understand.**

As they read to gather evidence to support their plan and argue against others, students can work within their groups to **evaluate the main ideas** of a particular reading, using their own words to **summarize** and **retell** the themes, ideas, and facts that they have gathered. In the course of their readings and discussions, the students will **acquire new words and articulate their meanings** within the contexts of their plans and proposals, demonstrating an operational understanding of their new vocabulary.

Finally, each group makes a presentation on its plan to a mock land-use board. The group presents the benefits of its plan and uses the evidence it has gathered to highlight the drawbacks of others. After the presentations have been made, the board votes to adopt just one plan. After the outcome has been decided, students can use the decision as a framework for **reflecting** on their reading and research strategies. By asking themselves the questions included in the reading comprehension prompts below, among others, students can see new ways to refine their research strategies to make them more effective in the future.

Teachers can begin by distributing to students an explicit list of **reading comprehension prompts** that they can use to guide their own progress. (The list is given below and also can be photocopied from the Appendix, p. 148.) In introducing the prompts, the teacher discusses the prompts with students, explicitly models each technique, then coaches students as they practice using the prompts in class. With a few demonstrations and reminders from the teacher, most students will be able to apply the strategies on their own to become increasingly independent readers. However, the teacher should be prepared to work for a longer time with smaller groups of students who still need to be coached in using the technique.

Reading Comprehension Prompts for Students

- **Predicting:**

    With a title like this, what is this reading probably about?

    What will happen next? (Turn to your partner and tell what might happen.)

- **Reflective questioning before reading:**

    Why am I reading this?

    Why does the author think I should read this?

    What do I expect to learn from reading this?

    How does this relate to my life?

    What do I already know about this topic?

- **Reflective questioning after reading**:

    What do I still not understand?

    What do I still want to know?

    What questions do I still have about this topic?

- **Evaluating**:

    What is the most important idea that the author presents? Why?

    If I were the author, what would I say is the main point I was trying to make?

- **Paraphrasing or retelling**:

    What was the reading about?

    Can I explain to my partner or group, in my own words, the meaning of what I just read?

    (The group or class also can engage in "group retelling," with one student beginning and others picking up where the previous speaker leaves off.)

- **Summarizing**:

    Can I identify all the key concepts from the reading and write a summary using these concepts?

- **Identifying words and meanings**:

    Does that word or passage make sense? Why or why not?

    Can I find something about the passage that can help me make sense of it?

    Do I know something about an unfamiliar word or its context that can help me understand what it means?

- **Reflecting on reading strategy**:

    If I were to read this again, what would I do differently knowing what I know now?

    What helped most in figuring out what was confusing or unclear?

    What other things could I have done?

These guidelines for students have been shown to work well, but teachers should feel free to adapt and customize the prompts to suit specific groups or activities.

It should be clear that these strategies encourage students to pay close attention to science content while building their language skills. As a result, students learn more science as they grow in language ability.

Strategies for Explicit Teaching in Reading

Reciprocal teaching

This modeling strategy (Vaca, Vaca, and Gove 1995) lays the foundation for later metacognitive techniques that can be personalized by each student. "Reciprocal Teaching . . . is designed to improve students' reading comprehension by helping them explicate, elaborate, and monitor their understanding as they read," notes the National Resource Council (Donovan, Bransford, and Pellegrino 1999). "The model for using the metacognitive strategies is provided initially by the teacher, and students practice and discuss the strategies as they learn to use them. Ultimately, students are able to prompt themselves and monitor their own comprehension without teacher support."

In Reciprocal Teaching (p. 149) teachers model a particular technique that students can use to learn on their own to improve their comprehension. The method is reciprocal because the teacher and students exchange roles during their discussions about how to understand written material.

The activity begins with an unfamiliar science content reading. The teacher explains that the group will concentrate on four areas related to the reading:

- formulating questions to be answered by the reading;
- clarifying parts of the reading that are hard to understand;
- summarizing what has been read; and
- predicting what the next section of the reading will discuss.

As an introduction, the teacher looks over the material to be read and talks aloud about her thoughts: "What's this about? Why does the author think this is worth reading? What's the main idea?" As students come to use the strategy more easily and confidently, they can contribute their own questions to make the list a group effort instead of just the teacher's.

After that introduction, the teacher and group silently read the first passage or section of the text. Afterward, the teacher demonstrates for students how she approaches the four tasks.

First, the teacher frames questions: "What did the author mean by . . . ?"

Second, the teacher searches for ways to clarify difficult or unclear passages: "In the previous paragraph, the author says something that helps me understand his reasoning here" or "I see from the diagram that in this sentence the author is really saying that. . . ."

Third, the teacher summarizes what has been read: "So the author is saying. . . ."

Finally, the teacher predicts what the next section will be about: "Based on what was just said, next the author probably will explain. . . ."

As the teacher thinks aloud, students join in to help her answer the questions, clarify difficult passages, construct or revise the summary, and sharpen her predictions.

After the teacher leads a few such discussions, students take over. The group reads another passage, then a student takes on the four tasks. The teacher becomes part of the group learning from, and helping clarify, the student's thinking processes.

If a student struggles, the teacher can prompt the student with questions such as "Why did that strategy work for you in understanding what the author meant?" or "Why did you go to that passage to help clarify this one?" The teacher should offer praise and sincere encouragement, as well as constructive criticism, to students who are having trouble mastering the techniques.

Throughout, the teacher and students should abide by the **four rules** that guide Reciprocal Teaching:

1. **Rule for good questions**: They are clear and stand by themselves.

2. **Rule for clarifying:** Look for incomplete information, unclear references, unusual expressions, and words that are difficult or unfamiliar. The teacher should be prepared to spot-check for understanding; students often will think or assume that they understand a concept or relationship when a little dialogue with the teacher will show that they do not.

3. **Rule for summarizing**: Look for the topic sentence, make up a topic sentence if none exists, and omit what is unimportant. The topic sentence helps students define for themselves, and then summarize, the reading's main themes and ideas.

4. **Rule for predicting**: Use the title and the headings, the author's questions in the text if there are any, and the author's structure of the material. (For example, perhaps the author mentions in passing "two kinds of birds" or "four levels of habitat"; in the next section, he probably will provide details.) Teachers should encourage students to look ahead in the reading and to use chapter titles and subheadings to anticipate the author's ideas.

Students can take notes on the strategies the teacher models, or the teacher can give students sheets detailing the strategies and the four rules (see Appendix). Having seen the techniques in action, and having the notes or handouts to use as prompts, students then can use the four steps them-selves when reading new material. With occasional reminders from the teacher, students can internalize these steps and use them until they become subconscious habits.

After students have begun to benefit from the techniques they learn through Reciprocal Teaching, teachers can broaden the strategy and apply it to student metacognition.

Pre-reading questions

As students gain confidence and skill in using metacognitive strategies, teachers can ask students to pose specific questions to themselves about the content of a reading before they begin to read. The self-generated questions give each student a personal investment in making sense of, and finding meaning in, the text. The strategy builds on the foundation of independence students gained through Reciprocal Teaching and helps them strengthen their reading comprehension and extend their independence even more.

In applying this strategy, each student generates a list of questions about a reading before beginning it. Instead of relying on the teacher's guidance or list of questions, the student now creates questions based on personal interest and curiosity. As with other metacognitive strategies, the teacher demonstrates the technique several times so students understand it well enough to use it effectively on their own.

Students begin by looking at the reading's title and table of contents. They then flip through the pages looking at subheadings, diagrams, or highlighted points. From this quick survey, each student prepares a list of personal questions to be answered while reading.

The search for answers to these personal questions imposes a structure on the text that is personally meaningful to each student, a necessity if the student is to genuinely learn from the reading. That structure enables each student to read with a purpose, a focus, and a direction that come from within the student, not solely from a teacher or a school requirement. By giving a personally meaningful structure and purpose to the act of reading, students are better able to comprehend what they read, forge a personal connection to it, and then apply the meaning to their own lives.

For example, students reading about the human genome might ask common questions such as "Why are all humans basically the same shape?" But one student in the group might ask, "Could I really clone myself? How would I go about doing that?" Another might want to know why a cousin suffers from a genetic condition that the student does not have, but wonders if it might develop later. Articulating these personal interests can help a student relate the content of the reading to her own life and, therefore, help her comprehend and internalize the facts and concepts being presented.

Students often raise another question that has personal consequence for them: "Is this reading too hard for me?" There is a little-known trick that teachers can give students to answer that question. The student begins to read a page in the material and places the little finger of one hand on the first unfamiliar word, the ring finger on the second, and so on. If the student uses the thumb before getting to the bottom of the page, the material is too difficult.

Searching for evidence

Students can use this outline as they read to identify scientific evidence in a reading (p. 150).

Students begin by formulating a hypothesis for which they expect the reading to provide supporting evidence. (For younger students, teachers can substitute easier words such as *idea* or *question* for *hypothesis*.) Then as they read, students write individual pieces of evidence into the outline template's first four sections: "facts," "statistics," "examples," and "expert authority." (Teachers can customize the outline's suggested categories to suit the kinds of evidence presented in a specific reading.) After finishing the reading, students write reflectively in the outline's fifth and final section to decide whether the evidence they have gathered from the reading has convinced them that the hypothesis is true. To do so, they can answer a series of questions: Am I convinced? Why or why not? If not, what other information do I need to convince me?

Before or after students write their conclusions, the teacher can lead students in a discussion of how complete and convincing the evidence was. Also, if the ideas presented in the reading are controversial among the students, the outlines can supply the evidence students can use as the basis for writing reports or essays.

Reading for evidence also can help students understand how to analyze different kinds of evidence and their relative importance. For example, students could read news accounts of research claiming that adding prune extract to hamburger meat can kill 90 percent of all *Escherichia coli* bacteria (which is dangerous to humans) without heating the meat. Students might state the hypothesis as a question: "Does adding prune extract to hamburger meat kill 90 percent of all *E. coli* bacteria?" Students then can sort information from the news accounts into the outline's five categories. Using this template reinforces the mutual alliance between the processes in reading and science.

Not only does the outline provide students with opportunities to develop critical reading skills, but it also helps them become sensitive to varying opinions, ideas, and points of view. Reading for evidence focuses students' attention by giving them a specific challenge to complete while reading. The technique also is transferable: students can use it to gather and evaluate evidence when reading material in subject areas other than science.

Write as You Read Science

This strategy helps students become more active readers by combining mental activity with a physical task. As they read, students identify key concepts, words, and passages in printed material and use pencils, colored highlighters, or sticky notes to identify portions of a text that they want to remember or don't understand. On a separate sheet of paper, they also write notes to themselves, questions about the text, and definitions of new words. As they work, the connection between physical and mental activity helps students remember the important ideas contained in what they read. Through the activity, students also create their own study guides for reviewing the material later.

To help students learn the technique, teachers at first can require that each student make a certain minimum number of comments or highlights per page. Also, students can share which passages they highlighted, which words they did not know, or the questions or disagreements with the text that they noted in the margins. By seeing how others use the method, students can become more comfortable and adept at using it themselves.

As many of us did in college, each student who regularly uses this technique will evolve a personal coding system of highlighting colors, abbreviations, and so on to quickly remember the significance of a marked passage. The following list of student guidelines (also on p. 152) is intended not as a set of rote instructions, but only as a guide to help students find their own ways of making texts personally meaningful.

Write as You Read Science: Guidelines for Students

1. Underline the main ideas or topics.
2. Underline the parts you want to remember.
3. Make a mark next to parts you do not understand.
4. Highlight the parts you find interesting.
5. Circle the parts you agree with.
6. Underline the parts your teacher wants you to know.
7. Write notes about information you want to remember to remind yourself why it is important to you.
8. Write questions about information you do not understand.

9. Write notes about your thoughts and feelings.

10. Write a short summary of the reading.

11. Write definitions of, or sentences with, words you do not know.

Graphic organizers

Graphic organizers provide visual learners with an additional aid in comprehending the meaning of what they read. It is important to remember that the function of graphic organizers is only to help students organize ideas from a reading more effectively; by themselves, graphic organizers do not necessarily help students *comprehend* what they read. With this additional tool, however, many students will be better able to apply other comprehension strategies. For that reason, graphic organizers are best used as a supplement to the techniques of Reciprocal Teaching, which equips students with comprehension strategies.

There are many such devices that teachers can choose among. We suggest three as examples: the Herringbone Graphic (Walker 1992), concept mapping, and Venn diagrams.

The **Herringbone Graphic** (Figure 4–1) parses the ideas in a reading the way that diagramming a sentence parses its words. Students start with a picture resembling a fish skeleton. As students read, they note the answer to one question about the reading on each rib of the skeleton: who, what, when, where, how, and why. When they have all the answers, the teacher shows students how to combine them to compose a sentence expressing the

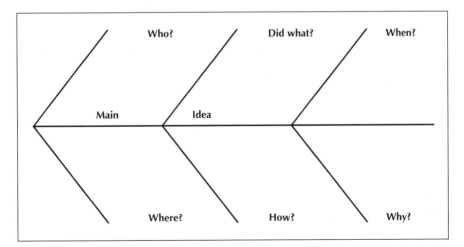

Figure 4–1. *Herringbone Graphic*

reading's main idea. The sentence can be written along the skeleton's spine. (Alternatively, the main idea can be written along the skeleton's spine, then the secondary answers filled in later along the ribs.)

The Herringbone Graphic also can structure a discussion of the reading, with students and teachers comparing their answers to questions and explaining their reasoning.

Concept mapping (Figure 4–2) is another graphic organizer that students can use to highlight and weave together the main points within a reading. The method allows students to brainstorm about the big and small ideas that they have encountered in the material and helps them (especially if they are visual learners) comprehend not only the reading's ideas but also their relationships.

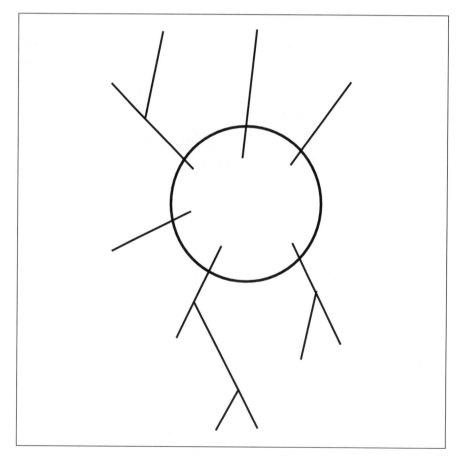

Figure 4–2. *Concept Mapping*

If the technique is being used by a group, the teacher draws a circle on the board. In the circle, the teacher writes the reading's subject or main theme. Students then call out the main ideas and subpoints of the reading, each response sparking others. Each response is written in its own circle that orbits the center circle containing the subject or main theme. As students discuss the relationship of the ideas, the teacher draws lines from the center to the main ideas, among main ideas, and from main ideas to related subpoints. Soon, students have a map of the reading's structure of ideas and a diagram of how those ideas bear on one another. Individual students can use the technique, too, but a group discussion tends to elicit a more complete picture, at least until students are thoroughly familiar with the technique and are able to use it effectively. At that point, students can use concept mapping (in full-class sessions or in small groups) in other literacy-related science activities such as preparing presentations or analyzing media messages.

Venn diagrams (Figure 4–3) are an additional tool that students can use to develop the skills of comparing and contrasting.

Two partially overlapping circles are drawn, each representing one of the elements being compared or contrasted—a basset hound and an Irish setter, for example. The students can begin by naming properties or attributes of each dog: the basset hound has short legs, short fur, and a black and white coat; the Irish setter has long fur, a reddish-golden color, and stands tall. Students can jot each trait of each animal on a sticky note and then stick it inside the appropriate circle of the diagram. Then the notes that are the same in each

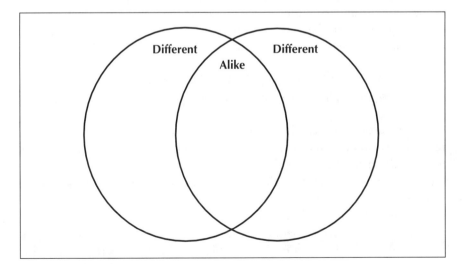

Figure 4–3. *Venn Diagram*

circle ("dog," "mammal," and "four legs," for example) can be moved to the section of the diagram where the two circles overlap.

Venn diagrams also can help students understand more sophisticated relationships between two ideas or objects by comparing and contrasting them using criteria that the students decide. Using the diagram helps students identify the characteristics of each separately, then discover the ways in which the two subjects are alike. The graphic is a tool that students can use to understand each subject in greater detail as well as to clarify the similarities, differences, and relationship between the two. As students become more adept at this task, they can use the graphic without the aid of the sticky notes.

In upper grades, Venn diagrams can serve more sophisticated purposes. The graphic can be used to compare and contrast complex ideas from a reading, such as different theories about a natural process or differing solutions to the same problem, and determine what they have in common and precisely how they differ. Similarly, Venn diagrams can be used as a negotiation strategy to clarify or resolve debates: where two opposing positions overlap, there is agreement and, therefore, the basis for constructive discussion.

Conclusion: Leading Students to Read with Awareness

If students are to improve their comprehension in reading science content, they must understand on a visceral level that reading is not just collecting discrete pieces of information but also the ability to synthesize those pieces into a complete, deep, and personally meaningful understanding. That process goes far beyond just understanding words and leads to what is often referred to as "enduring understanding" (Wiggins and McTighe 1998). To achieve enduring understanding, every student needs to

- become aware of her own reading habits; and
- master the strategies that good readers apply naturally or intuitively.

After articulating explicit performance expectations for comprehension, teachers and students then can select metacognitive techniques and strategies for explicit teaching that are tailored to enable students to achieve those expectations. By applying the strategies and techniques in inquiry-based activities, students can practice their new understandings until they reach for the new tools without having to think about it.

Ultimately, when students are able to combine metacognitive strategies and personal reflection, they begin to be able to see their own performance with some degree of objectivity. With that ability, they can identify differences in their reading performance as they progress. Metacognitive strategies empower them; an ability to assess their own improvement energizes them and propels them in an ongoing search for personal excellence.

At that point, students become self-directed readers—capable of independent comprehension—and free the teacher from the repetitive policing actions that characterize so many conventional approaches to instruction.

5

Writing
Paths to Clear Expression

When teachers treat students as serious learners and serve as coaches rather than judges, students come to understand and apply standards of good scientific practice.

—NATIONAL SCIENCE EDUCATION STANDARDS

Guided inquiry in science often involves as much writing as reading. Even in more conventional instructional approaches, science students regularly write reports of various kinds. Consequently, most students will have adequate, and some will have ample, opportunities in the normal course of their science activities to improve their writing skills.

Students and teachers should distinguish between two purposes of writing. What might be called **presentational writing**—in lab reports, for example—is, in effect, a performance for the benefit of others: in it, students use their best writing skills to communicate information they possess to another person as clearly and concisely as they can. Conversely, in **exploratory writing,** students are writing to and for themselves. They use written language in their science journals and similarly less formal venues as a tool to "listen to themselves think." As they write reflectively about their experiences, data and evidence they have gathered, and their reactions to them, students use words to mold the facts and concepts they have learned into an articulated, personal understanding of an aspect of the natural world.

Teachers can invest a relatively small amount of time to capitalize on such opportunities by helping students adopt good writing habits early. In that way, the teaching strategies for writing also are **metacognitive:** they are designed to help students reflect on the process of writing and cultivate the habits that good writers practice naturally.

Some of the strategies will be applied differently in different grades. Elementary teachers may teach basic writing strategies formally as part of language activities, then coach students to apply the strategies when writing about science or any other subject. In upper grades, where subjects are seg-regated, a science teacher may have good enough relationships with language teachers to encourage them to add these metacognitive writing strategies to their language programs. If language teachers use them as well, science teach-ers and language teachers can reinforce each other's efforts. In any case, it is wise to confer with language teachers about their grade-specific writing goals and their suggestions for incorporating other writing strategies into the science program. Collaborating with language teachers not only builds good-will among professionals teaching in different curricular areas but also helps coordinate and create synergies among teaching strategies.

Performance Expectations for Writing

Students learning science write narratives of laboratory procedures they have conducted, they write in science journals, and—especially in guided inquiry—they write persuasive essays that call upon them to organize and argue from the evidence they have gathered in their investigations. Each kind of writing carries its own performance expectations.

That need not be cumbersome to either the teacher or the student. Per-formance expectations for each kind of writing are slight variations on this generic set of criteria for good writing (p. 154).

Generic Performance Expectations for Writing. The student:

- **Establishes a context that holds the attention of the reader.** Do I show the reader why the written piece is interesting enough that it should be read?
- **Develops an overall idea that clearly expresses a personal point of view about the subject.** Is my controlling idea simple (such as "this is what I did and why")? Do I use my controlling idea to determine the organization and content of my writing?
- **Includes appropriate facts and details.** Do I include all necessary information to fully explain my controlling idea?
- **Leaves out unnecessary and inappropriate information.** Do I leave out all information that does not support or contribute to the reader's understanding of my controlling idea?

- **Provides an ending or closing to the writing.** Do I include a summary or other satisfying ending to my writing?

Performance expectations for any specific kind of writing assume, and are based on, these five principles.

Presentational writing

For many students, presentational writing in formal reports is the most common writing assignment in science classrooms. Performance expectations for presentational writing can be adapted to reflect the specific goals of any given assignment. However, despite the particular nature of any individual presentational writing assignment, all should meet certain basic criteria (p. 155).

Performance Expectations for Presentational Writing. The student:

- **Records, organizes, and conveys information accurately.**
- **Includes relevant details** such as scenarios, definitions, and examples.
- **Anticipates readers' problems, possible mistakes, and misunderstandings** and offers additional information and guidance.
- **Uses a variety of formatting techniques** such as headings and subheadings, logical structures, graphics, and color, all to make it easier for the reader to understand the information being communicated.
- **Writes in a voice** consistent with the document's purpose.
- **Employs word choices** consistent with the document's purpose and appropriate for the intended audience.

For example, in the Mystery Spill, discussed in Chapter 2, students can write a final report explaining the steps they followed to figure out the category of substance spilled on the classroom floor. The Fruitvale Story also presents an opportunity for students to write this kind of summary report.

Narrative procedures and lab reports

These are special forms of presentational writing and, therefore, require their own set of performance expectations.

In guided-inquiry classes as well as in conventional science programs, students write narratives of the step-by-step procedures they conduct in their investigations. The object of the report is not only to make a formal presentation explaining what was done, but also to explain the procedure in such thorough detail that anyone else could use the report as a scientific recipe to replicate the procedure and reach the same result. In a narrative procedure or lab report, every relevant detail must be noted clearly, thoroughly, and in the correct sequence.

The novel *Cantor's Dilemma,* written by world-renowned biochemist Carl Djerassi, illustrates the vital link between good science and the precise use of language. In the book, a scientist devises an experiment that ultimately proves his revolutionary new theory of how cancer tumors form and he publishes a preliminary notice of his results. But his lab assistant keeps sloppy records of the experiment. A leading cancer scientist uses the notes to try to replicate, and thus authenticate, the discovery but cannot. The second scientist's inability to verify the discovery threatens to ruin the discoverer's professional credibility.

"'He drums it into everybody's head in the lab: 'Write up your experimental work in sufficient detail so that anybody can duplicate it,'" the remorseful assistant says. "'If there's one lesson to be learned from this experience, it's that even the smallest details should be put into one's notebook. You never know which details may turn out to be crucial'"(Djerassi 1989). (This and Djerassi's novel *I, Cantor* are excellent windows into the human side of science.)

The following metacognitive checklist for students (p. 156) can help them learn to avoid the lab assistant's mistake.

Performance Expectations for Narrative Procedures and Lab Reports. The student:

- **Engages the reader.**

  Have I written an introduction?

  How does the writing interest the reader in the procedure?

  Is the organization and detail of the writing suitable to the reader's purpose in learning about the procedure? For example, do I want the reader simply to understand the procedure or to be able to perform it?

- **Provides a guide for the procedure that anticipates the reader's needs.**

  Do I use simple language?

  Do I define words that the reader might not know?

  Do I break the procedure into enough steps to make it easy to understand? What transitional words do I use to help the reader follow the sequence of procedure (*first, second, finally,* etc.)?

- **Uses appropriate writing strategies.**

  Do I include enough information for the reader to complete the procedure?

Do I arrange ideas in the order in which the steps of the procedure should be carried out?

- **Includes relevant information.**

  What information does the reader need, and need to understand, in order to perform the procedure?

- **Excludes unnecessary information.**

  Do I write about things that are not part of the procedure?

  Do I include unnecessary information?

- **Provides a closing or ending** to the writing.

  Do I include a summary or conclusion at the end?

The Mystery Spill activity in Chapter 2 showcases the importance of this aspect of literacy in science. In the activity, students conduct an investigation to determine the kind of substance that has been accidentally spilled on the classroom floor. As part of the investigation, students must categorize the nature of the hazard that the spilled substance represents. (As noted in Chapter 2, this activity is a simulation of a real investigation but uses harmless materials.)

A teacher could assess students' procedural understanding and their literacy skills at the same time by asking each student to write a narrative procedure or lab report that someone unfamiliar with the process could use to conduct the same investigation. Alternatively, or in addition, students could write a procedure for an investigation that they would like to undertake. (Designing an investigation or experiment is not only an essential skill in science but also an important element of inquiry-based science learning.) Writing procedures requires precision in the use of language, careful attention to detail and sequence, and a clear explanation of how to draw the correct conclusion. All are essential skills in science: if a scientist cannot communicate the precise details of a procedure and the conclusion drawn from it, the scientist's work cannot be replicated or confirmed.

In the narrative, students would **engage readers,** perhaps by asking, "If a truck spills a substance on the street in front of your house, how do you know whether the spill is dangerous to you and your family?" Teachers then can determine whether the student's subsequent explanation **uses simple language, defines technical terms adequately,** and **includes all necessary details while excluding the irrelevant.** In doing so, the teacher can be gauging the student's level of skill with language while assessing the student's understanding of the activity's scientific content and procedure. In this activity, the skills of language and the expression of an understanding of science are indivisible.

Exploratory writing

In guided inquiry, exploratory writing is an essential tool that students use to figure out just what they learned and what it means to them. The most common venue for students' exploratory writing is the science journal.

The science journal is more than a record of data that students collect, facts they learn, and procedures they conduct. It also is a record of a student's reflections, questions, speculations, decisions, and conclusions, all structured by a controlling idea—which, in the Fruitvale activity, is "What's in the water and what do we do about it?" The journal enables students to use a framework of science ideas and activities as a venue for improving writing. As such, the journal is a central place where language, data, and experience work together to fashion the student into a better scientist.

As a record of the student's simultaneous improvement in science and language, the journal serves as the teacher's window into a student's understanding of science and the student's ability to express that understanding. For example, if the data or procedures recorded in the diary are inaccurate, the teacher would know immediately that the student is weak in procedural or mathematical skills. If the procedures and data are accurate but the expression is weak, the teacher would know that the student's problem lies more in a lack of ability to draw conclusions or to express them adequately.

To help students express their findings and ideas as clearly as possible, many teachers give students a list of performance expectations to paste in their journals as a writing guide (p. 154). The expectations tell the students what the teacher expects to see in a well-written journal. More important, the list helps students understand what good exploratory writing is and how they can achieve it in their journal entries and elsewhere.

To help students internalize what they learn, the performance expectations are preceded by two questions that students can use as prompts for reflection. Teachers can customize the questions to suit specific activities. For most activities, the following questions can serve as generic examples:

- What new ideas or insights did I gain after today's reading or investigation?
- How can I use what I have learned in my everyday life?

Guided by those questions, students can use the following personal performance expectations as a guide in exploring their ideas through writing. Although we use science journal entries as an example, the same guidelines can be applied or adapted to other forms of exploratory writing.

Exploratory Writing and Science Journal Entries: Guidelines for Students

When I write in my science journal, I will use these questions to help me focus my ideas:

1. **What new ideas or insights do I have now after studying this section?**
2. **How will I use what I have learned in my everyday life?**

When I write in my science journal, I will

- begin my writing by describing briefly what we did;
- express my ideas and my point of view about what we learned;
- include all the important facts and details about what we learned;
- leave out all the unnecessary and unimportant information; and
- provide a closing to my journal entry.

As noted earlier, teachers can tailor the questions to the content, structure, and goals of individual science lessons or activities. However, the teacher should take care to provide explicit questions in order to focus students' writing.

The Fruitvale Story, described in Chapter 2, is an activity that has been structured for students to keep journals. The activity unfolds over several days. Each day, the students learn a little more.

One day, they learn that people in the town of Fruitvale have started drinking bottled water because they fear that the town's water supply may be contaminated. The contaminant may be coming from a chemical company that makes pesticides, a farm that uses pesticides, or a housing development that has used pesticide on its land. Students can record these facts in their journals and also may jot down questions they want to pursue, such as "Is the slope of the land from the chemical plant to the well important?" On other days, students conduct investigations that help them understand the concepts of parts per million and parts per billion and the range of time it takes for liquid to pass through different kinds of ground materials.

Students conduct an investigation that mimics the process of testing water from three different wells around Fruitvale for pesticide contamination and then determine the concentration of the contaminant in different wells. Using the data, they choose another three well locations to test. In their journals, they can record their reasoning about which wells to test first. They also can record the resulting data and reason from it to choose another three wells to test. When a well does not yield the results expected (the spot might be sealed from outside contamination by a clay deposit, or perhaps errors were made in collecting the sample), the student can hypothesize about why the results turned out unexpectedly, record questions still needing to be answered, and record the chain of logic that leads to modifications of the drilling plan. Finally, students use the class' collective test results to map the contamination plume and determine its source.

Throughout the activity, the student's journal is a strategic learning tool. In their journals, students use language to explain to themselves the meaning of the data collected. "Why is the pesticide concentrated in parts per million at a well farther from the farm when a closer well shows a concentration of parts per billion?" "My three well tests didn't turn out the way I thought they would; why not?" "Which well locations should we test next?" The journal becomes a record of the way a student uses language to parse a scientific issue, to reason about it, and to master scientific principles and processes.

Student Metacognition Strategies for Writing

As noted previously, metacognition is a process by which students recognize and alter their own mental habits and approaches to learning by using performance expectations, self-awareness prompts, and teachers' examples and models of effective learning strategies. However, metacognitive strategies take students beyond the performance expectations to deeper levels of reflection and personal understanding.

For example, students engage in exploratory writing in their science journals throughout their investigation of water quality in Fruitvale. Their exploratory writing is shaped by their consideration of the guiding questions listed previously. But metacognitive strategies, which the teacher can model, lead students to more probing questions about the reasons and choices underlying their finished writing. Students can ask themselves how useful their writing strategies were, which they would change or keep, and why. They can share their exploratory writing with peers, helping each other analyze how effective their reasons and choices were. These exchanges enrich students' understandings of their problem-solving procedures and choices as writers by enabling them to gather reactions and suggestions from a variety of readers. Students also can pick up useful tips from their fellow writers and glimpse effective habits of mind that others use. Such conversations can help students gauge their progress in the use of metacognition when writing.

The performance expectations for presentational writing, coupled with sessions of reflection and conversation, similarly can help students compare the results intended with those achieved. Teachers can design and model reflective questions to help students determine how well their narrative procedures, lab reports, and other presentational writing meet relevant performance objectives. Using those questions, students can conduct a personal review of the completeness and satisfaction they feel when reading what they have written—an internal conversation that becomes the first step in discovering how they can improve their writing. Then they can discuss the quality and effectiveness of their writing with peers.

Reflective conversations and internal reviews can be centered around such considerations as "What really surprised me about writing this was . . ." "When I look at my other journal writing, I think this piece is different because . . ." and "I think this piece of writing is strong (or weak) because. . . ."

Through this kind of reflection, students maximize personal meaning not only from what they have written but also from their experience of writing it. Metacognitive strategies and regular reflection chart the path that leads students to understand how they can improve steadily and independently over time.

Strategies for Explicit Teaching in Writing

Structured Note-Taking

Students can use this transitional metacognitive strategy (Figure 5–1) to bridge the gap between reading and writing.

As students read and research in preparation to write, they take notes. But students frequently are mystified by what effective note-taking looks like and how to use notes to write a coherent report. Often, they simply copy information from a book or the Internet and end up with unrelated scraps of information that they do not quite know how to organize.

As outlined by Buehl (2001), Structured Note-Taking gives students a graphic organizer to help them wrest order from informational chaos. In Buehl's example, students are learning about endangered animals. As the students begin to take notes, they write the name of an animal—say, "dolphin"—in the center of a sheet of paper. They then draw a line up from the name, ending at a box in which the students write a question: "What kind of problem is the animal having?", in the case of the dolphin. Students learn from their research that one answer is "Dolphins are being caught in underwater tuna nets and killed." They write that answer next to the boxed question. Next to that boxed question is another, such as "Who or what is causing the problem?" Students find the answer to that question and note it in a similar way. Other lines radiate out from "dolphin," leading to questions such as "Where does this animal live?" and "What can be done to help this animal?," which can be

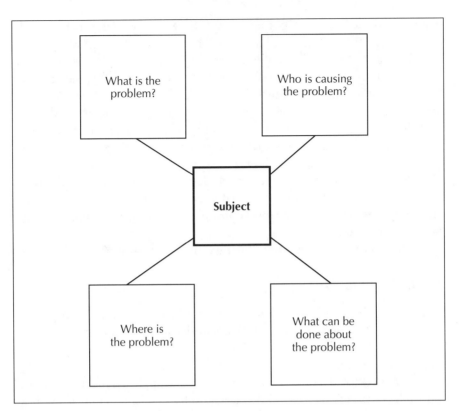

Figure 5–1. *Template for Structured Note-Taking*

answered in the same way. (A copy of the graphic organizer for Structured Note-Taking is included in the Appendix, p. 159.)

As students become comfortable using Structured Note-Taking, they might want to adapt concept mapping or other graphic organizers to help them organize their notes before writing. They also might design their own graphic organizers tailored to the kind of research they are conducting or report they are writing. Eventually, as students internalize an understanding of how to relate and organize information, teachers might guide them toward other, perhaps more traditional, outlining techniques.

In another strategy for Structured Note-Taking, students can generate lists of questions that occur to them as they read research material. Then, for each question, students use notes from their reading to write a brief general response and follow it with specific supporting details.

For example, perhaps students are reading about the likelihood of human space travel in the twenty-first century. As they read, they could write down questions that occur to them, such as "What do I already know about space that might make human space travel difficult?" As they read more, they would discover that distances in space are vast. They also would learn that there is no evidence of life as we know it elsewhere in the universe. They would go on to find additional data, such as the limitations on spacecraft speeds and the hostility of other planets to human life if we could reach them. Students can think of, and write down, their questions both before and during reading.

To organize these notes before writing a report, students can write each question on a separate index card, with each card having three parts: the question, the general response, and the specific details.

As they prepare to draft a report, students can lay out all the index cards in front of them and compare them to decide which pieces of information are most important and which are most appropriate to the introduction, the body of the report, and the conclusion.

Students can use either note-taking technique in groups or individually.

The Writing Checklist

This is a step-by-step guide to the five stages of creating a published piece of writing. It, too, is metacognitive: students work alone or in groups to internalize a process that enables them to continue to analyze their work independently and improve on their own.

The checklist's steps are generic in nature and apply to report writing and most other writing tasks that students encounter in science. (Journal writing, which is less formal, more exploratory, and not intended for publication, should not be held to these same formal standards.) Each student can keep a copy of the checklist (p. 160) in the science notebook and the teacher can use a slightly different version (p. 161) to monitor students' work in groups as well as individually.

The writing checklist helps students understand that formal writing is a five-step process. Suggest to them that they permanently attach the checklist to their science notebooks or folders or in some other place where it will be easily accessible as a reference. Discuss with students each step in the checklist.

Using the Writing Checklist: A Guide for Teachers

1. **Prewriting:** Students develop their ideas using brainstorming techniques such as concept mapping. They think about ways to organize and plan their work.

2. **Drafting:** Each student writes a rough draft, getting down as many ideas as possible. Remind students that revising and editing come later; what is important in this stage is to include anything that might be important. Also, remind students that they will proofread and make spelling and grammatical corrections later, during the editing phase.

3. **Revising:** In groups of four to six, students take turns constructively critiquing one another's work.

   - First, a student reads his work aloud and others in the group give a collective oral summary of what the student has written.

   - Second, listeners discuss the strengths of the writing (or compliment the author on some aspect of the work).

   - Next, listeners ask questions about any parts of the writing that are unclear.

   - Then listeners make constructive suggestions to improve the writing.

   - Finally, authors revise their writing by adding, deleting, or rewriting. They review and reread their writing to make sure that it makes sense.

   As part of this metacognitive strategy, students edit and proofread one another's work—tasks usually shouldered by the teacher. Students often learn more during freewheeling interchanges of comments and critiques with peers than from either the hasty notes that teachers write on students' papers or during more structured (and often one-way) discussions with teachers about their work. The interchanges not only help students become better writers by putting them in direct contact with critical readers but also strengthen students' group process skills.

   Of course, group critiques are not always possible every time anyone writes something. Students also should gain practice in revising their work on their own. But that can come later. A few early sessions of collective critiques can help students learn to view their own work more critically and then to revise it more effectively when they work alone. In that way, working together helps students learn individually.

4. **Editing:** Students proofread their writing to correct errors in grammar and spelling. If students seem to need extra help, review some simple editing rules, such as those for capitalization and punctuation. Have students meet in pairs to check each other's editing.

5. **Publishing:** After students write the final draft, they might want to illustrate their work or otherwise enhance the text before others see it. In any case, the point of writing is to share ideas with others. Students can publish a class anthology or a science newsletter for their parents or other students.

Teachers are urged to photocopy the following list from the Appendix (p. 160) and give it to students. Students can use the list as a template for consistency and improvement in their writing.

Using the Writing Checklist: A Guide for Students

1. **Prewriting:**

    I have thought about all the elements I want to include in my writing.

    I brainstormed ideas for my writing using concept mapping or a similar method.

    I made a plan for how the parts of my writing will fit together.

2. **Drafting:**

    I wrote a rough draft including all of the ideas I brainstormed and anything else I thought of while I was writing that might be important.

3. **Revising:**

    I checked that my writing makes sense.

    I read my writing in a student reading conference.

    I listened to my peers' suggestions and used those I thought would improve my writing.

    I made at least one change in my draft, taking special care to remove ideas and statements that are not relevant or important.

4. **Editing:**

    I proofread my work to make sure I used capital letters to begin names and sentences.

    I checked to make sure that I used the right punctuation and that every sentence ends with a period or a question mark.

    I proofread my work for correct spelling.

    If I wrote using a computer, I used the spell-checking and grammar-checking programs to alert me to possible mistakes.

    I exchanged my work with another student for a final reading.

5. **Publishing:**

    I produced my final draft of the text.

    I illustrated my final draft in any way that was necessary or useful.

    I made my writing available to an audience.

Group interactive reports

Group interactive reports (see Appendix pp. 162–163) enable students to talk in small groups about their ideas after completing an activity but before writing about it. The method allows students to clarify their thinking about a particular experience and to learn from each other. It also sharpens their overall writing, oral, and group process skills. For students daunted by the processes of writing, group work eases their transition from spoken to written language.

In groups, students discuss what they have learned or observed in an investigation, what they can infer from their data, and what conclusions they can draw. One student serves as a recorder who writes down the group's ideas, while all members of the group use concept mapping (described in Chapter 4) or a similar technique to collect and structure their ideas. Then the students in each group work collaboratively to write a report, using the writing checklist to organize and guide their work.

It is essential in writing a group interactive report that every member of the group agrees on each sentence included in the report. This mandate for consensus strengthens students' skills of collaboration and also enables each student to clarify and confirm her accurate understanding of the facts and ideas they have studied. By using the performance expectations for speaking, listening, and group interactions detailed in Chapter 6, students shape a collaborative, final written or oral report of their work. Alternatively, individual students in the group can use the consensus list to write their own reports, blending the interactive skills of speaking and listening with the more individualized skills of writing.

As an example, group interactive reports are used in an investigation called Product Life Cycle, an activity module being developed by the Science Education for Public Understanding Program, based at the University of California at Berkeley. In the activity, students study methods of waste disposal used by different municipalities and then develop a plan for waste management for their own county. To create their plans, students work in small groups.

First, each group discusses possible ways to manage various kinds of waste. Students use concept mapping to brainstorm ideas they want to include in their plan. Second, after the discussion (where group interaction strategies might be applied and assessed), each group follows the guidelines for group interactive reports, as well as the writing checklist detailed earlier, to draft, revise, and edit a group report. The groups exchange their reports to elicit others' ideas, responses, and editing suggestions to make the final versions as complete and readable as possible. The final step is publication of the group report.

Group Interactive Reports: A Guide for Teachers

1. Before student groups begin work, review the performance expectations for writing. Be sure each group has a copy to refer to.

2. Ensure that group members select one person to record the group's ideas.

3. Remind students that each group member is to contribute ideas to the report and that each member is responsible for encouraging reluctant contributors. (The teacher may need to demonstrate for students some effective ways to do this.)

4. Remind students that before any sentence is included in the report, the recorder receives agreement from each member of the group.

5. If there are study questions at the end of the activity, they can be used to guide the content of the report.

6. After the groups have completed their rough drafts, review the writing checklist (discussed previously) with students to make sure that they understand how to turn the rough draft into a final version.

Group Interactive Reports: A Guide for Students

1. Select one person to record the group's ideas.

2. All members of the group are to contribute ideas to the report. Each group member is responsible for encouraging those who are reluctant.

3. Before any sentence is included in the report, every member of the group must agree on the sentence.

4. Use study questions in the learning materials as a guide in shaping the report's content.

5. Use the performance expectations for writing as a guide in structuring and drafting the report.

6. After completing the rough draft and consulting with the teacher, use the writing checklist to prepare the report's final draft.

Writing narrative procedures and lab reports

As noted earlier, laboratory procedures are an essential process in science. A narrative procedure or lab report is a step-by-step account of a scientific experiment or investigation. The account can then be used by others as a set of sequential instructions to use to replicate and verify the investigation's results (see Appendix p. 157).

Especially in elementary grades, students often write procedures in the first person: "First, I got some vinegar. Then I put 10 drops into Cup A." Writing in the first person lures students into the procedure by helping them form a personal connection with it.

To understand why writing in the first person is useful, it is necessary to consider the way in which children acquire speech. When a child first learns to speak, the speech is ego-centered; the child narrates events and describes and explains the world through a first-person perspective. When the child first learns to write, the tendency toward first-person narration pervades the writing. Analytical forms of speaking and writing develop later, as students evolve from more concrete, limited levels of perceiving and functioning to more abstract and formal operational skills. At that point, students are ready to take a more detached perspective in writing or speaking.

Because of this developmental sequence, students are better able to write narratively (in the first person) than analytically because narrative writing draws upon their natural strength in expressive language. Later, as students become more adept at writing lab reports and other narrative procedures, the teacher can help them make the transition from a casual approach to the more formal third-person format.

Writing procedures is an integral part of science and, therefore, of learning science. Scientists use these sets of instructions to plan their laboratory work and to record the procedures they conduct so that colleagues can reproduce the work exactly when attempting to confirm any resulting discoveries. Because writing procedures lies at the heart of laboratory science, students should have opportunities to write them both as planning tools for lab work and as records of experiments that they have conducted.

A procedure is a recipe of scientific discovery. As in any recipe, the writing must be clear, complete, and exact or the result will be flawed. For that reason, writing the narrative of a procedure not only brings students into contact with the essence of science but also taxes their skills in written language.

When students write a narrative lab report, there are four basic questions they need to answer. Teachers can photocopy the list of these questions from the Appendix and give it to students to guide their work. (The questions should shape the narrative but need not be restated within the report.) Because these questions guide the writing of all procedures, students can follow this template when they use other procedure-writing structures, including the third-person voice.

Writing Narrative Procedures and Lab Reports: A Guide for Students

1. **What was I looking for?** Describe the research question you were trying to answer or the prediction or hypothesis you were testing.

2. **How did I look for it?** Describe what you did to answer the research question or test the prediction or hypothesis. Include a description of the method and materials you used.

3. **What did I find?** Describe any observations you made and the data you collected.

4. **What does this mean?** Formulate a conclusion based on the data you collected. Discuss your predictions and their accuracy and how the data supported your hypothesis.

To put students in the right frame of mind, teachers can suggest that they think of the report as a letter they are writing to a friend who was not in class but who must now conduct the procedure on his own.

3-2-1

This technique (p. 164), which I helped create for use in a variety of inquiry-oriented science activities, has two purposes. First, it helps students understand the difference between observation and inference, a distinction essential in science. Second, it can serve as a student's first step in planning self-designed investigations and drafting narrative procedures for them.

In 3-2-1, students first observe an event, then draw an inference from their observations, and finally pose questions for further investigation that their observations and inferences raise.

In one popular 3-2-1 inquiry, the teacher makes a "smoking machine" from a plastic soda bottle stuffed with cotton. A cigarette is fitted into the bottle's neck and is "smoked" by squeezing the bottle. The students observe that as more of the cigarette is smoked, the cotton becomes blacker.

The logical inference is that the more a person smokes, the blacker the lungs become. This inference often leads students to ask why anyone decides to smoke. More than a rhetorical question, the query can become the seed of students' own investigations into why people choose to smoke despite the known health risks involved. With that question as a starting point, students then can draft a narrative procedure mapping the course of their investigations.

In addition, 3-2-1 provides teacher and student with a window into the student's understanding of the concepts underlying an inquiry. The method also links the processes of scientific observation and inference with the exploratory and reflective powers of language.

Real Science

This approach combines exploratory and presentational writing and helps students connect issues in science and technology to their own lives. It was developed by Marc Siciliano, the director of the Math, Science, and Technology Academy at Chicago's Lake View High School.

In Real Science, students begin by reading a news article about an issue in science and technology. Working alone or in small groups, students then write a three-paragraph essay expressing their understanding of, and reaction to, the article. The essay's first paragraph identifies the issue or issues that the article is about. The second details the evidence the article offers to support the issue presented. In the final paragraph, students give their opinions about the issue and describe how it relates to them personally. Siciliano calls the three steps **issues, evidence, and you** after a yearlong guided-inquiry science course of the same name (SEPUP 1996).

In presenting the essay structure to students, teachers can give them the following guidelines (p. 165).

Real Science: Issues, Evidence, and You

1. **Issues. What is the article about?** After reading the article, decide what the focus of the article is. That is the issue. There may be one or several issues within an article. The issues may be clear or they may require you to analyze what is written and draw conclusions.

2. **Evidence. What facts and expert opinions are given to support and strengthen the issues?** After deciding what the issue is (or issues are), write down the evidence in the article that helps convince you about the issue. In this paragraph, you will state the facts that support the article and reinforce the arguments.

3. **You. What does this article mean to you and how does it apply to your life?** This paragraph is the true purpose of the assignment. Once you have identified issues and found evidence to support them, you must react to the issues and the evidence. Give your opinion and focus on yourself. Be creative and explain your feelings and viewpoint about these real-life issues. Use the evidence in the previous paragraph to support your conclusions.

Creative writing

Imagination plays a central role in science. By writing imaginatively, yet with focus and discipline, students can expand their experiences and skills of science as they strengthen their abilities to use language. There are forms of creative science writing appropriate to all grade levels.

For example, in lower grades students can meld the skills of language and scientific observation by writing poetry. This often is a sticking point for science teachers in upper grades, though: poetry is for language class, not science class. However, there are two short poetic forms, haiku and cinquain, that lend themselves quite well to developing students' abilities to observe natural phenomena. Still, a significant number of middle and high school science teachers are skeptical of taking class or homework time for students to exercise their literary imaginations. Therefore, a poetic approach to science is often easier to implement in lower grades where teachers are accustomed to integrating disciplines. Cinquains are typically used in elementary grades only, while haiku can be effective through early middle school.

The essence of haiku (HY-koo) and cinquain (SIN-kwain) is close observation of natural phenomena coupled with the concise and accurate use of language, two attributes that are equally essential in any kind of science. Poetry also prompts students to play with, and listen more closely to, language, which, in turn, helps them expand their ability to think creatively.

The forms take advantage of children's curiosity about nature to develop science skills. For example, writing poetry is another activity that can help students learn the difference between observation and inference. A student might be tempted to "observe" that a flower likes sunshine because the flower raises its face to the light. The teacher can point out that there is no physical evidence that the flower has emotions; instead, the poet—like the scientist—records physical details and reports them concisely and accurately to the reader. Conducting extended observations to write their poems also can help students lengthen and strengthen their attention spans, another key element in science or any form of learning.

Haiku poetry originated in seventeenth-century Japan. A haiku is three short lines that express a perception about a natural object or phenomenon—clouds, grasshoppers, or spring growth, for example. The first line is fixed at five syllables in length, the second line has seven syllables, and the final line has another five syllables. An example of a student's haiku (Whitten 1997):

> The sun is setting.
> Bright orange sky is fading.
> The black sky is here.

A cinquain poem also is concise. The first line is a single word that names the object or event in nature that is the poem's subject. The second line is two words that describe an attribute of the subject. The third line, three words long, describes the subject's actions. The four-word fourth line expands the third line's description. The fifth and final line is one word, expressing the poet's subjective response to the subject. An example (Thier 2001):

> Snow,
> Silently falling,
> Ground covered anew,
> White, glistening, clear sunlight,
> Refreshing.

The first step in writing nature poetry is to go outdoors. (Poetry writing is a good excuse to get students outside without a more formal agenda such as playing a sport.) Students can work alone or in pairs to observe a creature or an event for an extended time. (Teachers should be prepared that many students may need to be shown how to look closely at an object and make observations.) If students work in pairs, they can stimulate and enhance each other's perceptions.

Whether alone or in pairs, students can brainstorm observations much as they do in concept mapping. They can record their observations in sentence fragments to keep up with the pace of their perceptions. Back in class, students can work together or individually to create their poems. Teachers may wish to create a customized version of the writing checklist, detailed earlier, to help students draft and revise their poems.

In another creative use of language, students can read extra material, write reports, or make presentations that explore the human side of science. Students can learn about the struggles, false turns, self-doubts, and controversies that underlie scientists' great discoveries. For example, students often are surprised to learn that Einstein had problems in school or that Galileo was almost put to death for announcing that Earth moves through space. The story of the brouhaha surrounding the announcement of "cold fusion" in 1989 also reveals much about the inner workings of professional science.

Using creative language to explore science's human dimensions helps students learn about science's history, processes, and seminal figures and discoveries. But, just as important, it also shows students that science is a human activity, filled not just with equations and procedures but also with surprises, mysteries, and the full range of human motivations and emotions. Students can research the development of a scientific theory or the life story of a great scientist and write reports or make presentations about what they have learned. (As an example, see the biography *Glenn Seaborg: Elements of a Life*, p. 176.)

Indeed, creative writing, whether poetry or prose, shows students that science is not a rote exercise but one that can be more engrossing than any movie or mystery novel. As the *National Science Education Standards* points out, experiencing the "excitement and personal fulfillment" of science is just as important in students' science education as learning concepts and formulas (National Academy of Science 1996).

Conclusion: Writing for Understanding

Language, more than mathematics, is the tool by which students articulate and explain science facts and ideas to each other, to teachers, to parents, and to others in their communities.

Students can discover their own understandings of ideas through **exploratory** writing in science journals and other less formal venues. There, students have the freedom to use words the way a portrait painter uses pencil lines: to test an arrangement of ideas before formalizing it. If the arrangement is not quite right, the artist will erase the lines and try others in a slightly different pattern. Similarly, students can cross out or throw away the words that do not quite articulate their understanding and try others until their words reflect their thoughts precisely. Exploratory writing is a process of thinking and thus of discovery.

Once students have clarified their understandings through exploratory writing, they are better able to write effectively in **presentational** forms such as narrative procedures and formal reports.

Through strategies for explicit teaching embedded in inquiry-based activities, teachers can help students recognize and apply the metacognitive techniques that they can use to learn to improve their writing independent of a teacher's supervision.

6

Speaking and Listening
Paths to Clear Understanding

Reading and writing should flow on a sea of talk.
—JAMES BRITTON

In our society and economy, successful group work is at least as important as individual performance. For group work to be efficient as well as effective, group members must be able to communicate concisely and accurately. That means being able to speak and listen just as clearly and accurately as they read and write. Student work groups in science—particularly in the inquiry-based classroom—are a natural venue for teachers to help students practice and enhance their oral, and aural, literacy.

As there are in writing, there are two categories of speaking and listening. One deals with exploratory speech, the other with presentational speech.

Exploratory speech includes the spontaneous exchanges among students in work groups and between students and teacher. Students use exploratory speech to experiment with ideas so they can focus their thinking. In contrast, students use **presentational speech** to share their conclusions with others in a more prepared and formal way. Therefore, presentational speech requires a different set of performance expectations. Students also can use the performance expectations for the two kinds of speaking and listening as metacognitive tools to gauge and improve their own performance.

Exploratory Speaking and Listening

The importance of exploratory speech—what appears to be simple conversation—in science classes cannot be overestimated. We discover and sharpen

75

our own ideas by talking about them and seeing how other people react, a crucial element of learning that Harlen (2000) calls "negotiated meaning."

When participating in discussions, students can use the performance expectations for exploratory speech (p. 166) not only to guide their own behavior but also to gauge that of others. Looking at their peers as models (both good and bad) helps students hone their metacognitive awareness of their own speaking and listening habits. They then can combine that awareness with the performance expectations for exploratory speech to improve their own speaking and listening abilities.

In contrast, formal oral presentations demand a higher degree of organization and forethought than casual or spontaneous conversations. Performance expectations in this category (p. 166) can serve as metacognitive prompts to help students prepare presentations that engage the listener as well as persuade or convey information effectively. The teacher can use these criteria to evaluate a student's performance as a speaker at the same time the teacher is assessing the presentation's science content. In guided inquiry, formal presentations often are a culminating activity through which teachers determine how well students have understood, internalized, and integrated the material they have studied.

Not all presentational speaking is rigidly structured. Occasionally, as in role playing, students can have prepared presentations that cover specific themes or talking points but then must field questions from an audience or deal with challenges to their points of view. Such situations require students to improvise, which requires the use of exploratory speech within a prepared framework. Performance objectives and teaching strategies can be adjusted to fit the situation.

As noted earlier, this chapter also suggests performance expectations and teaching methods for two increasingly important categories of speaking and listening: group interaction and persuasive strategies. These are forms of speaking and listening that require the "negotiated meaning" (Harlen 2000) that leads students to reformulate their ideas by listening to others and finding the appropriate words to convey their ideas as part of the group. For that reason, group interaction and persuasive strategies are included as part of this chapter. However, the same performance expectations, and the metacognitive strategies that the expectations highlight, can be applied to written forms of group interaction (circulating drafts of a controversial report for editing and comments, for example) and persuasion (such as newspapers' opinion columns about science-related issues). The skills and expectations related to persuasive strategies also often can be applied in activities that involve media analysis.

Performance Expectations for Exploratory Speaking and Listening. The student:

- **Initiates new topics and responds to topics initiated by others.** When the teacher or a member of the student's work group finishes discussing a particular subject, the student might say, "That reminds me of a story in the newspaper last week." Being able to make links between the current subject being discussed and related areas confirms that the student has listened and understood.

- **Asks relevant questions.** If the questions are relevant, not only has the student clearly been listening but also has understood what others have said.

- **Responds to questions with appropriate explanation and details.** If the student's elaboration or comments are relevant, the student has listened to what others have said and understood it.

- **Uses language cues to indicate different levels of certainty.** The student uses phrases such as "what if," "very likely," and "I'm not sure whether." Students should understand that change, and therefore uncertainty, is the essence of science and scientists use these language cues when they think and speak.

- **Confirms understanding by restating or paraphrasing what others have said.** Paraphrasing goes beyond mere explaining and is not possible if the student has not understood and internalized the concepts being discussed. Paraphrasing also helps students coalesce their own thoughts and ideas.

Teachers can go beyond explaining these expectations to students and model the concepts in the teachers' own interactions with the class. The teacher also can monitor students' degrees of clarity in speaking while strolling among student groups as they work, listening to the students interact and joining the conversations where appropriate. (See the section on running records later in this chapter.)

My Sweet Tooth is an activity that is rich in student conversations, both as they work in groups to examine the sweeteners' physical properties and as they discuss and debate which sweetener each student would choose to use. The conversations offer concentrated opportunities for students to practice the skills identified by these performance expectations and for teachers to assess individual students' use of them.

In these discussions, the students typically **initiate new topics** in response to comments from others. One student might say, "Sugar rots your teeth," prompting another to comment, "But artificial sweeteners are bad for you."

The exchanges lead students to **ask relevant questions** ("How do you know artificial sweeteners are bad for you?") and cause them to **elaborate** ("I read about a scientific study that says so. It says that . . ."). Students then might **test their understanding by paraphrasing** what the student has said about the study and talk about their **levels of certainty** regarding the study's conclusions—or their levels of uncertainty when they realize that the evidence might not be as compelling as the student supposed.

An efficient way for teachers to keep track of students' progress or problems is through the use of Running Records, a technique adapted from the Reading Recovery program. In this form of embedded observation, the teacher circulates among students conducting an activity. She records observations regarding each student's specific performance in group interaction, exploratory speaking and listening, or other targeted literacy skill as the student confronts a particular concept or process. The teacher could list specific traits expressed in the performance expectations on one side of a page and make notes on each student on the other side. (Some projects are developing Running Record software for handheld personal digital assistants.) Running Records as a strategy for teachers is discussed in more detail later.

Performance Expectations for Presentational Speaking. The student:

- **Shapes information to achieve a particular purpose and to appeal to the interests and background knowledge of audience members.** For example, students should understand the difference between an explanatory and a persuasive presentation and structure their data and arguments accordingly. An effective presentation also addresses the audience members "where they are" intellectually and does not use information that is irrelevant to, or beyond the grasp of, listeners.

- **Shapes content and organization according to its importance and impact.** The information included in the presentation is not limited to information and resources that are easily available.

  Speakers ask themselves the key question, "How do I want what I say to affect my listeners?" With the answer to that question in mind, the speaker does not prepare a presentation merely by reading an encyclopedia entry on a subject but researches thoroughly to ferret out information necessary to make the presentation complete and effective to a specific audience that has a particular background and point of view.

- **Uses notes and other memory aids to structure the presentation.** "Winging it" from memory shows a lack of respect for the audience as well as for the material.

- **Develops several main points relating to a single idea.** The student uses organizational techniques that keep the presentation focused on its subject from beginning to end.

- **Engages the audience with appropriate verbal cues and eye contact.** Students must understand that their physical presence and behavior during a presentation can be fundamental factors in determining how an audience reacts to a presentation.

- **Projects a sense of individuality and personality in selecting, organizing, and presenting material.** Projecting a personality engages the audience and gives listeners an initial reason to listen to what is being said.

Listening to presentational speech

Shared with students, these performance expectations (p. 167) can help students gain the most from listening to an oral presentation. Again, the teacher can model these expectations in responding to presentations.

Performance Expectations for Listening to Presentational Speech. The student:

- **Takes notes about important information and details.**

- **Identifies arguments that are illogical, unreasonable, or do not make sense.** Especially by taking notes, students can identify inconsistencies, instances of overgeneralization, and other instances of fallacious reasoning such as inferring causation from correlation.

- **Accurately summarizes the central idea of the speaker's remarks.**

- **Forms an opinion about the issues under discussion.** Did the speaker present all necessary information to make his case or to enable the audience to understand the subject?

The Fruitvale Story provides a good context for making and listening to oral presentations. At the end of the activity, students attend a mock town meeting where various approaches to decontaminating the town's water supply are debated. As Fruitvale citizens, students make oral presentations on behalf of their preferred solutions. To be persuasive, they must **shape their information and argument according to an overriding purpose** and **be thorough in researching and providing information.** They must prepare their presentations by **targeting the interests of the audience** and **using notes to remember key points.** Finally, they must **engage the audience** as they speak, doing so in part by **projecting their own personalities.**

Students acting as council members must listen well enough to probe the strengths, weaknesses, and effectiveness of the ideas and persuasive structure within each presentation, as must other students in the audience, in order to rebut arguments against their own positions.

While assessing students' understanding of the activity's science content, the teacher also can gauge students' abilities to use language to articulate, defend, question, and demonstrate an understanding of a point of view derived from evidence.

Group Interaction

Increasingly in science classrooms, and especially in guided inquiry, students work in groups. Group work is successful only when students interact effectively. That means that students must be able to articulate ideas as well as to listen carefully enough to understand clearly what others are saying. (The world might well be a more peaceful place if national leaders abided by these same performance expectations!)

Group interaction demands special skills—and, therefore, its own set of performance expectations—that normal conversation does not (p. 168). In group interaction, students speak and listen, but within the context of continuous interplay among group members and between themselves and the group. Group interaction is a specialized form of listening and speaking because it is many-sided as well as being continuous and freewheeling: each individual filters what others say through his personal perceptions of reality as well as his own interpretation of what has been said. But, unlike regular conversation that makes the same demands, group interaction also calls for instant analysis, comprehension, judgment, and response without the luxury of time for reflection.

By following a few guidelines for the exploratory speech and listening that define group interaction (p. 169), a student work group can become an ongoing group metacognitive process: students can use the same performance expectations to assess their own behavior and those of their groupmates. Teachers can use the same guidelines as performance expectations when observing student groups.

Performance Expectations for Group Interaction. The student:

- **Takes turns,** adopting and relinquishing tasks and roles appropriately.
- **Actively solicits others' comments and opinions.** The student recognizes that successful group work results from the participation and contributions of every member.

- **Offers own opinions forcefully** but without dominating. The student understands the difference between being assertive and being overbearing.
- **Responds appropriately** to comments and questions. The student is courteous, able to modulate the give-and-take of discussion, and uses the listening skills outlined previously.
- **Volunteers contributions and responds when asked** by the teacher or peers. The student understands that group members must contribute constructively.
- **Expands on responses** when asked to do so and gives group members similar opportunities.
- **Is able to use evidence and give reasons** in support of opinions expressed.
- **Employs group decision-making techniques,** such as brainstorming or an appropriate problem-solving sequence, such as recognizing a problem, defining it, identifying possible solutions, selecting the optimal solution, implementing the solution, and then evaluating the result.
- **Works with other group members to divide labor** in order to achieve overall group goals efficiently.

The activity My Sweet Tooth embodies the kinds of student interactions that characterize guided inquiry. In the activity, students first work in groups to examine and list the physical properties of the sweeteners. Because the task must be completed within the time allowed, students can **divide labor** by splitting the group into pairs, with each pair of students examining only one or two of the sweeteners involved. In each group, the students will discuss, compare, and contrast their observations as they record them.

The activity also asks students to discuss and debate the advantages and drawbacks of using each kind of sweetener. These negotiations give ample opportunities for students to **offer their own opinions, solicit each other's comments,** and **challenge others' views and respond to their challenges using evidence.** Throughout the activity, the students find chances to **take turns, participate without dominating,** and abide by the other expectations that mark an effective group session.

Running Records: A Tool for Teachers

Running Records (p. 170) are a quick, relatively easy way for a teacher to note on the spot how well students are meeting performance expectations for group interaction. Marie Clay refers to Running Records as "a tool for coding, scoring, and analyzing a child's precise reading behaviours" (1993). However, the same technique can be adapted and used in conjunction with the performance expectations for speaking, listening, and group interaction. The technique enables teachers to document the behavior of individual students as it occurs, then analyze and reflect on it later. In addition, keeping Running Records also sharpens a teacher's ability to observe and recognize productive student behavior in context.

For example, to use Running Records to note students' behaviors during group interactions the teacher lists the students' names down the left edge of a sheet of paper. Across the top, the teacher creates column headings for each of the nine performance expectations for group interaction. When a student demonstrates a certain behavior, the teacher jots one of five symbols in the appropriate column across from the student's name:

✓—   demonstrates the behavior independently most of the time

S—   sometimes demonstrates the behavior independently

R—   demonstrates the behavior only when reminded

N—   does not demonstrate the behavior at all

0—   no opportunity during this activity to demonstrate this behavior

Once a teacher is comfortable using the method, it becomes a quick, practical, and particularly useful tool during students' exploratory speaking and listening sessions. Teachers can use their notes not only to track students' growth over time but also to target specific interventions for individual students having trouble learning specific behaviors.

Persuasive Strategies

Science will play an increasingly central role in the lives of today's students after they leave school. As citizens, they will be called upon to make evidence-based judgments and express their views. Language is the framework within which tomorrow's science-based public issues will be structured and decided as various factions use language artfully to persuade others to their points of view.

For that reason, students should gain experience in making and evaluating evidence-based arguments on behalf of particular points of view, both as formal presentations and in a more spontaneous, exploratory framework (p. 171).

Performance Expectations for Using Persuasive Strategies. The student:

- **Engages the audience** by establishing a context, creating a voice, and otherwise creating reader interest.
- **Develops a controlling idea that makes a clear and knowledgeable judgment based on evidence.**
- **Includes appropriate information and arguments to support the main idea.**
- **Excludes irrelevant information and arguments.**
- **Anticipates and addresses reader concerns, counterarguments, or other points of view.**
- **Supports arguments with detailed evidence, citing sources of information as appropriate.**
- **Provides a summary or closing to the argument, clearly stating conclusions.**

Again, The Fruitvale Story is an excellent context for helping students improve their persuasive skills. After students have drawn their conclusions about the source of the contamination in the town's water, they devise their own remediation plans. Students then can write letters to (or editorials for) the Fruitvale newspaper reasoning from the evidence they have gathered to support or oppose a particular solution. The writings can be effective, evidence-based arguments only to the extent to which they employ the seven strategies or expectations noted here. Students can use the same persuasive strategies in preparing to argue for their chosen plans in front of the Fruitvale town council (a panel of students and/or teachers). The teacher can evaluate a student's performance in the seven persuasive strategies at the same time the teacher is assessing the student's grasp of relevant science concepts and how well she is able to make those concepts a part of her own internal thought processes.

Student Metacognition Strategies for Speaking and Listening

As noted, metacognitive strategies evolve from performance expectations as a way for students to become aware of their own habits of thought and approaches to learning. Similarly, the strategies can help students assess their own progress in achieving the expectations.

Students can use performance expectations and metacognition strategies to focus their personal reflections about their speaking and listening experiences and to use those reflections as tools for personal improvement. To help them articulate their reflections, the teacher can invite students to talk about a communication problem that arose, or that they expect to arise, in their work group.

For example, they could share their frustrations arising from a recent group debate in which they tried to persuade their peers about the advantages of allowing the federal government to fund stem cell research. They could talk about the variety of perspectives that emerged and how hard it was to get others in the group to understand their point of view. The teacher can help students move past their frustrations and to identify ways to avoid or solve similar problems in the future. In other words, students can explain how they used the performance expectations for listening and speaking, and their metacognition strategies, to monitor their approaches and problem-solving processes and to ponder how they worked. When students reflect in groups facilitated by the teacher, they learn about one another's strategies and their effectiveness. Engaging in reflective dialogue with peers not only enhances students' communication skills but also helps them assess their progress toward becoming more effective receivers and communicators of concepts.

Strategies for Explicit Teaching in Speaking and Listening

Guided inquiry gives science students plenty of opportunities to speak and listen as part of regular classroom activities. Students can use exploratory speech to sort through and clarify their understandings and ideas, then turn to the techniques of presentational speech to organize, record, and demonstrate their new knowledge.

Teaching strategies for presentational speech are well known: teachers ask students to prepare and make oral presentations. Students making presentations can use the relevant performance expectations to help them prepare; students and teachers can use performance expectations for listening to presentational speech to critique and evaluate students' performance and guide them toward improvement.

In contrast, students build their skills in exploratory speech when conversation is unstructured—when students are free to follow ideas wherever they lead, even to dead ends or mistaken conclusions. Exploratory speech necessarily leads to exploratory thinking: students try out ideas, listen to others' reactions, and modify or extend their own understandings as a result.

As a teaching strategy, exploratory speech often works best when teachers don't "teach," but rather when they create an environment that encourages students to engage in free-flowing conversation. In these contexts, the teacher's role is to do as little as possible other than keeping students focused on the subject and ensuring constructive exchanges among them.

Self-directed exploratory speaking and thinking develops students' ability to use evidence to defend or modify ideas. Exploratory conversations also strengthen students' skills in using evidence to defend or modify inferences and conclusions. The give-and-take of discussion helps students gain experience in careful listening, using persuasive strategies, and working successfully as part of a group. Finally, exploratory speech builds their social skills and self-confidence. Students in classrooms where group discussions regularly convene find more meaning in their studies while they also grow socially and emotionally (Harlen 2000; Scott 1992).

For those reasons, the strategies in this section concentrate on exploratory, rather than presentational, speaking and listening.

Shared Inquiry in Science

This strategy, created for the CHEM 2 program (SEPUP 1997), blends meta-cognitive strategies with Socratic discussion methods.

Students sit in a circle and engage in a dialogue centered on a reading in science, with the teacher moderating and facilitating the conversation. To seed the dialogue, the teacher asks open-ended questions about the reading that challenge students to make inferences about the text's deeper meanings. As students attempt to answer those questions, they confront additional ones that they must grapple with. Students are encouraged to speak directly to each other instead of to the teacher. The teacher's role is to help students develop the skills and confidence that will enable them to conduct meaningful discussions on their own. As the group becomes accustomed to the interchanges, the teacher no longer needs to be the center of the conversation.

The activity's purpose is threefold.

First, the discussions encourage students to think beyond the written word and to delve into the written material's deeper ideas and meanings. The dialogue helps students integrate their ideas with those of the author and to internalize those ideas so students can apply them in variable and complex real-life contexts.

Second, as students work to clarify and defend their ideas, their skills in reading comprehension, exploratory speech, and listening for understanding grow along with their understanding of the reading.

Third, students' exploration of the text's deeper meanings strengthens literacy skills such as the ability to infer and to draw conclusions. The analysis that Socratic dialogue prompts also helps students cultivate higher-level thinking skills.

In the discussion, students agree and disagree on various points, using the text as evidence to support their ideas. The teacher prods students—and students challenge each other—to analyze and reflect on their own ideas. Students see that others taking part in the discussion, including the teacher, are sincerely struggling to better understand the text. They also learn that there is no single right answer to many of the questions posed. In the course of the discussion, students can learn that reasonable people need not agree on everything—and that, when views differ, evidence becomes the most powerful persuasive element.

If the activity has succeeded, students will not want to end the conversation when the bell rings and the teacher will hear them continuing to debate and share their ideas as they walk out the classroom door.

To organize a session of shared inquiry (pp. 172–173), the teacher can pair students' usual four-person work groups to make groups of eight students. Each group reads the text and then generates three or four divergent questions based on the reading. For example, Lynne Cherry's book *A River Ran Wild* (1992) chronicles the history of a piece of land along a river from Native American days through settlement, urbanization, despoilment, and finally a campaign to restore the river and its ecosystem. In one class, the book sparked these divergent questions:

- If you were an early inhabitant of the area, how would you react to the river slowly dying?
- Was there a difference in the goals of Native Americans and white settlers?
- In what ways did the people coming later live differently from the early inhabitants?
- How can one person's vision be an effective catalyst for change?
- Was progress taking place here? Why or why not?
- What is progress? How would you know it?
- Why do people like products, but at the same time do not like the processes by which those products are made?

The divergent questions formulated by the groups then can be discussed by the class as a whole.

Creating a Climate for Shared Inquiry Discussions

1. Ask students to sit in a circle.
2. Tell them that you will ask questions that reflect your uncertainty about various aspects of the material's meaning. Explain what you mean.
3. Explain that all students will be called upon to participate because everyone's ideas contribute to the group's understanding of the

material. That is, all students must contribute because the group needs as many points of view as possible to understand the material's meaning.

4. Present and explain the rules for shared-inquiry discussions.

5. Help students feel confident about sharing ideas. Do not evaluate students' ideas.

Rules for Shared-Inquiry Discussions

1. The teacher is a fellow inquirer, not an instructor, and does not state opinions or evaluate those expressed by students.

2. The teacher or discussion leader asks divergent questions to which there are many "right" answers.

3. Only people who have read the text may take part in the discussion.

4. The discussion covers only the material that everyone has read.

5. Discussion leaders may only ask questions, not answer them.

6. Students sit in a circle and speak directly to one another.

7. Speakers use passages from the text as evidence to support or challenge points of view.

8. No one can cite third-party opinions about the material ("Einstein once wrote about this subject and he says that . . .") without backing up the outside opinion with evidence from the written material.

9. Teachers or discussion leaders use reflective listening techniques, such as paraphrasing to confirm understanding, that make students feel comfortable and confident enough to express their ideas.

10. Students save their personal questions until the end of the discussion.

11. Each student may occasionally "pass" when asked to respond to a question (but not too often).

Conclusion: Improving Interactions with and Between Students

The pace and complexity of life are increasing at home and at work. In many situations, it is impractical to wait to circulate a memo or draft a report in order to communicate one's ideas to others. Yet spoken language is too easily mangled by the speaker and misunderstood by the listener. An impression created in a moment can take weeks of effort to eradicate, as teachers well know if they have worked with students who have formed mistaken impressions in class about scientific concepts.

The performance expectations presented here for exploratory and presentational speaking and listening can help students understand the elements of clear spoken communication and techniques for effective listening in a variety of venues. Students and teachers then can use the expectations for formal and informal oral communications to evolve metacognitive and explicit teaching strategies to cultivate speaking and listening skills in guided classroom activities. In the course of those activities, students also will have opportunities to develop and refine their abilities to work in groups, to persuade others, and to evaluate others' attempts to persuade them.

Even in textbook-centered classrooms, science presents students and teachers with many topics to explore through discussion and debate as well as through formal presentations. Classrooms rich in structured discussion also are rich in learning.

7

Media Literacy
Paths to Awareness

Media literacy is not so much a finite body of knowledge but rather a skill, a process, a way of thinking that, like reading comprehension, is always evolving.

—ELIZABETH THOMAN

Analyzing media messages, a skill also known as "media literacy," has become increasingly important in the context of science. Some experts tell us that genetically modified foods are a boon to health while other experts say that eating genetically modified foods is a foolhardy risk. Some experts tell us that we should take an array of vitamin and mineral supplements to ensure our health while others insist that such supplements largely are a waste of money.

To analyze these contradictory claims and make evidence-based personal decisions, a person must be familiar with the facts and processes of science. But that person also needs to be able to recognize and understand *how* those facts and processes are being presented and manipulated to put the best light on a given point of view. As Elizabeth Thoman, executive director of the Los Angeles–based Center for Media Literacy, points out, "At the heart of media literacy is the principle of inquiry" (n.d.).

Indeed, when students view media messages and information analytically, they are cultivating the habit of a "healthy skepticism" that the *National Science Education Standards* considers essential to the nature of science: "Science distinguishes itself from other ways of knowing . . . through the use of empirical standards, logical arguments, and skepticism" (National Research Council 1996). A healthy skepticism requires a delicate balance between being

89

open to new ideas and also being doubtful of claims for which there is no clear and convincing evidence. In this way, media analysis fosters critical and, therefore, scientific thinking: students learn to rely on evidence to identify arguments—especially those on behalf of unusual claims—as either weak or credible. In doing so, they also learn to differentiate between claims that have scientific validity and those that do not.

The need for skills in analyzing media messages is not limited to adult life. Students as well as teachers and parents are assailed by science news stories that often are prepared by writers or reporters with little understanding of science's methods or meanings. Also, students increasingly are turning to the Internet's unfiltered information for use in their projects and presentations. The ability to critically assess that information's value has become a key skill in conducting a valid scientific investigation or project, in the classroom and in the laboratory.

After establishing student performance expectations for analyzing media messages (p. 174), teachers can select explicit teaching and metacognitive strategies and appropriate activities (some of which are suggested here) to help students develop the analytical habits of mind that mark a healthy skepticism.

Performance Expectations for Analyzing Media Messages

The student performance expectations for media analysis have been adapted for use in science programs. Although they fit naturally into guided-inquiry activities (because science is about questioning), teachers in textbook-centered programs can use them just as easily to lead students into critical discussions of news articles, advertisements that make scientific claims, and other media presentations.

Performance Expectations for Analyzing Media Messages. The student:

- **Demonstrates an awareness of the presence of media in the daily lives of most people.** Studies and test results, ads, and claims of all kinds have become ubiquitous. Many of us simply try to ignore them. The first step in analyzing messages is to be aware that they surround us and that they exist for a specific purpose.

- **Evaluates the role of media in focusing attention and in forming opinion.** Most people are surprised to learn how many of their attitudes are adopted from media messages. This can be especially true for students who are concerned with what's cool without necessarily understanding how something comes to be considered cool. (The classic case is the techniques that tobacco advertising has used to persuade young people to smoke.)

- **Determines the presence and role of subliminal messages in a media presentation or entertainment program.** Students need to be aware that informational messages (often unspoken) are contained within movies, television shows, and songs that appear to be merely entertaining. Subliminal messages also may be embedded in news reports, scientific studies, and other information that purports to be objective.

- **Analyzes the context for advertising or persuasion that a media presentation creates.** What elements represent advertising? What part do advertisers, media owners, and audiences play in determining a presentation's content or the subjects it presents or chooses not to present?

- **Uses explicit metacognitive criteria to analyze media messages.** (This list can be given to students for them to use as prompts until healthy skepticism becomes a habit.)

  Who created this article or message?

  What techniques are being used to attract my attention?

  Does the writer use words designed to stir up my emotions or influence my ideas?

  Does the writer think I already know something about this subject? How much factual information is included in the presentation?

  Is the article complete? Did the writer present enough information on the topic for the audience to be able to draw an informed conclusion? Does the writer disclose sources of information so readers or listeners can verify the information's accuracy independently?

  What information or points of view are *not* presented?

  How unbiased is the message?

  What ideologies and value messages are embedded in the presentation?

  Are data, statistics, and evidence presented completely? Does the evidence presented help support the ideas in the presentation?

These performance expectations are a key element in the final portion of the Beijing land planning activity described in Chapter 2. In the activity, students research, weigh, and argue on behalf of one of eight possible uses for two hundred unbuilt acres on the edge of the one of the world's largest cities. The student group backing a particular use of the land must research the economic, demographic, and environmental impact of the choice that they make. Students also must make a persuasive case for their chosen use before the city's planning board (made up of their fellow students). Board members, and students backing competing uses, can use the criteria listed here to listen for instances of factual manipulation, rhetorical sophistry, or faulty logic as students present their cases. Teachers can compare their analyses of the presentations with those of the students, enabling teacher and students to learn together to sharpen their awareness of media tactics.

Student Metacognition Strategies for Media Analysis

The ability to analyze or deconstruct media and its messages integrates students' metacognitive strategies from reading, writing, speaking, and listening. Because tomorrow's adults will receive most of their information about science and technology through media instead of through personal experience, media analysis also is a key metacognitive tool that students will take with them from school and use across a range of activities throughout their adult lives. Media literacy is not a body of knowledge, but a process and a way of thinking.

Metacognitive strategies for media analysis encompass the abilities to read and listen not only effectively but strategically: to be able to comprehend what is said but also to be able to ask who is saying it and for what purpose. Metacognitive strategies for writing and speaking help students understand how to avoid distorting the messages they create; strategies for persuasion help them understand some of the ways in which messages can so easily be distorted (or how to deliberately distort their own). When students have experience using persuasive strategies, they more readily understand how others use these techniques to try to influence opinions and perceptions.

The ability to recognize those tactics is crucial if students are to be able to steel themselves against the daily barrage of written, spoken, and graphic persuasive messages—and also if they are to prepare adequately for their roles as citizens in a democracy. The performance expectations for media analysis, coupled with the media analysis checklist and explicit teaching strategies provided in this chapter, can enable students to develop metacognitive habits of mind that become a sharply focused lens through which they can clearly view media messages and tactics.

Strategies for Explicit Teaching in Media Analysis

The skills of media analysis or media literacy grow directly from guided inquiry. Indeed, the two share a goal: in each, teachers help students think critically about information, its sources, and its explicit and implicit messages.

Learning to gather, filter, assess, and apply information is fundamental to science. Therefore, the same principles of inquiry that define good science also lie at the heart of media analysis. As students learn to deal with information in their scientific investigations, they can apply the same skills to the messages of popular culture that they confront in films, television, music, and advertising.

Also, because a rich mix of media is always part of the guided-inquiry science classroom, activities related to media analysis can strengthen students' specific skills in other forms of literacy as well.

In the science classroom, being "media literate" means that students are able to evaluate information about a science issue from a variety of sources— technical reports, television programs, newspapers, and others. It means that students are able to compare information from different media forms and presentations on the same topic. It also means that students know how to use media judiciously as part of an overall exploration of a science topic—for example, that they are able to synthesize new information by drawing on various sources and use a variety of media effectively to get their message across.

Because the skills that media literacy comprises already are embedded in inquiry-based science instruction, teachers can easily find a variety of teachable moments in an inquiry-based activity to raise the questions that will help students develop a critical approach to media and their messages.

For example, students must understand that a message's author or sponsor shapes the message's stylistic and informational content. A study of tobacco's dangers that is done by the U.S. Food and Drug Administration is likely to differ in its conclusions from one sponsored by a cigarette company, for example. Similarly, students need to recognize that the choice of language, symbols, images, and sound in a multimedia presentation can all be useful in determining a message's usefulness and credibility.

Teachers also can help students become aware that different media take different approaches to the same subject. A story about human cloning that appears in a supermarket tabloid must be read differently from an article on cloning in a technical journal, for example.

The following checklist (p. 175) suggests several questions that teachers and students can use together to develop the habit of media awareness and analysis. (Following the checklist, we offer examples of relevant activities.) This metacognitive checklist can be photocopied from the Appendix and given to students to guide their reflections and decisions. Teachers can modify the questions or add others to suit the needs of their students or classroom activities.

Media Analysis Checklist

1. Who is speaking and what is the speaker's purpose? Who has created, published, presented, or sponsored this message and why?

2. Who is the targeted audience? How can I tell? How is this message tailored to that audience?

3. How unbiased is the information or message?

4. Is the information complete? Does the author present enough information for the audience to make an informed decision?

5. Does the author cite sources of factual information included in the message?

6. What techniques are used to attract or hold my attention?

7. What kinds of words are being used? Is the writer using words chosen to stir emotion or sway ideas?

8. How much information does the writer or sponsor think I already know about this topic?

9. Are values or lifestyles being promoted? What does the message present as being good to own, do, or be? What is promoted as being "not good"?

10. Read between the lines. What is implied?

11. What information or points of view are excluded from the message?

12. Are data, statistics, and evidence presented completely? Does the evidence presented help support the ideas in the article?

Using these metacognitive strategies empowers students to exercise discretion in their responses to media and their messages and to better understand how to use various forms of media as resources to enhance their science learning.

Media analysis activities

Teachers will have no trouble devising activities that highlight media's various forms and levels of messages and information. We suggest three here as examples to spark readers' own imaginations.

Science teachers in upper grades can present students with scientific studies of the same issue that arrive at different conclusions—whether antioxidant vitamins and minerals slow the aging process or whether flu shots work, for example. (A particularly dramatic example is to contrast the studies produced by cigarette makers about tobacco's health effects with studies on the same subject carried out by independent researchers.) Teachers then can coach students as they use the criteria in the media analysis checklist to deconstruct each study's messages and techniques.

To introduce younger students to media analysis, a teacher can find magazine advertisements that make a claim purporting to be based on scientific evidence: this detergent gets clothes cleaner, this headache medicine works faster and is gentler to the stomach, and so on. The teacher can ask students to look at newspaper, magazine, or television commercials to find their own examples of other claims that may be suspect or inadequately supported. Students can then use the criteria detailed in the checklist for media analysis to dissect the messages' information and techniques.

In a more elaborate activity, the teacher can help students analyze news coverage of science and technology issues.

For example, the teacher might collect two newspaper articles on the subject of human cloning, one article taken from a daily newspaper and the other from a supermarket tabloid. (The comparison illustrates not only the value of healthy skepticism but also what science is and is not.) The differences in the headlines, subject, and tone of coverage could fuel a class discussion of the character of various forms of media and how media influence personal decision making. The teacher can ask students for examples of personal or societal decisions that they and their families had to make that were influenced by media and their messages—environmental regulation or buying a new car, for example.

Next, in groups of four, students reflect on the questions from the media analysis checklist. The teacher asks students to think about which criteria could help influence their decisions, either positively or negatively. Then, working in pairs, students use the criteria to analyze one or two news articles they have brought from home or that the teacher has supplied that cover scientific or technological issues. They analyze the articles to see

- which of the analysis criteria apply to each article;
- how a criterion applies; and
- in what ways the technique might influence their decision or their ability to make an informed decision.

Finally, the teacher can lead a classwide discussion of the importance of understanding media forms and strategies. As a closing activity, students can amend or add to the checklist of criteria for analyzing media messages.

These and other media analysis activities also give students opportunities to strengthen their other language skills by expressing their insights and discoveries through written reports, essays, or formal class presentations.

Integrating Literacy Skills Through Media Analysis

Media messages come in written, spoken, and graphic forms. Therefore, to be media literate, students must be adept at using the full range of literacy performance expectations and metacognitive skills to navigate the sea of messages—science-related and otherwise—designed to sway belief and manipulate emotion.

To analyze media critically, students need to be able to read "beneath" the words on a printed page or listen "behind" the words in a persuasive message. They must have the analytical tools to infer hidden meanings and tease out the implications of information presented to them. They need to understand how to look at, and what to look for in, media messages—to understand that printed, graphic, and spoken media often construct their messages using styles of grammar, syntax, and metaphor chosen not only to capture our attention but also often to bypass our critical faculties and appeal directly to our emotions.

In reading, for example, media literacy means having the skills and intellectual tools to do more than comprehend the meaning of the words on a page. It means being able to read strategically: to be able to use metacognitive skills to compare, synthesize, analyze, and draw conclusions from a passage of text. A media-literate student understands persuasive strategies and processes information from the reading through the filter of that understanding. The student then weaves the information into a coherent and comprehensible message and uses metacognitive strategies to determine the writer's purpose and intent. After probing the writer's attitude and motives, analyzing the message's credibility, and identifying overt or hidden bias, the strategic reader then decides how, or whether, the message meets a personal need in, or has a personal meaning for, the reader.

Using performance expectations, techniques learned through strategies for explicit teaching (including teacher modeling), and metacognition prompts, students of all ages can learn "age-appropriate skills that give them a new set of glasses with which they can 'read' their media culture" (Thoman n.d.).

Writing, especially writing persuasive messages, puts students on the other side of the media equation. Students can better understand how media messages are artfully constructed by writing newspaper editorials or letters to local newspapers expressing their views on scientific controversies such as global warming, human cloning, or stem cell research. Through these engaging activities, students gain practice combining evidence and persuasive language to incite, sway, and motivate readers. (Students often gain more insight into media techniques by playing devil's advocate—writing essays endorsing views they oppose.)

Students can learn a good deal about media techniques by assuming the mantle of media manipulators themselves. Students could use the Searching for Evidence template to state a hypothesis and then support it using only those facts, statistics, examples, and expert authorities that are favorable, ignoring all other relevant information. Teachers might encourage them to be as manipulative and biased as they can—to use colored language designed to inflame, write metaphors intended to manipulate or misdirect the reader, and embed hidden value messages.

Students also could use media's persuasive tricks to create an ad campaign to warn others about the dangers of smoking. The activity not only cultivates students' skills in using media persuasively but also can enlighten students about the construction of cigarette advertising campaigns—appealing to young people's perceived need for acceptance by others as well as creating the appearance of sophistication, and, of course, fun. (People in cigarette ads always seem to be laughing, sailing, or otherwise sharing good times.) Playing on these same perceived needs, students might design ads to lure their peers away from tobacco by using the same subtext of embedded value messages and viewpoints that cigarette ads contain.

Through that experience, students can become more adept at applying performance expectations and metacognition skills to recognize manipulative techniques directed at them. Coupling performance expectations for writing and persuasive strategies with the media analysis checklist, students can work together to heighten their awareness of media's means of persuasion.

Performance expectations, metacognition skills, and explicit teaching strategies for oral communication—especially listening—are no less important in analyzing media. Many, and perhaps most, people rely on radio and television, not newspapers, as their primary source of news. At the same time, studies indicate that spoken messages, especially when accompanied by powerful graphic images, are more likely to bypass people's higher-order analytical filters and communicate directly with our more deeply rooted emotions (Daviss 1992). The guidelines for listening provided by the performance expectations and metacognitive strategies can become students' first line of defense against false or incomplete media reports about scientific and technological controversies or breakthroughs.

Students can defend themselves against false or misleading reports or impressions by applying a healthy skepticism: knowing when and how to verify information, to check sources, to compare and contrast differing versions of the same story, and to recognize the phenomenon of "spin." The questions listed in the media analysis checklist help students cultivate the habits of healthy skepticism and give them a filter through which they can listen to media and its messages realistically.

Regardless of their techniques, most media messages are made out of language. Language also is the primary tool we use to communicate with ourselves as we make sense of our environment. Therefore, students (or any of us) cannot properly interpret media's messages, or resist their manipulative tactics, without a suite of well-developed language skills. The more questions students know to ask about a media presentation's use of language, the better able they are to develop the healthy skepticism that will enable them to resist media's wiles. The performance expectations and metacognitive strategies for all areas of literacy combine in media analysis to empower students to accept, reject, or modify persuasive information and, ultimately, to construct their own evidence-based understanding of the world.

Conclusion: Learning to Weigh Sources, Not Just Evidence

An analytical approach to evidence is essential in science and, increasingly, in our lives as workers and voting citizens. The world is no longer a place where people trust experts to process and hand down the information each of us needs to make sound personal and public policy decisions about issues involving science and technology. These days, we all have to be able to think like scientists. That ability includes a habit of healthy skepticism: a scientifically literate person knows to trust evidence when not only the evidence itself but also the source it comes from pass certain tests of objectivity and completeness.

The science program is perhaps the best venue in school for students to cultivate these habits of mind. It is here where they most routinely gather and weigh evidence. (Increasingly, students turn to the Internet—a torrent of unfiltered information—as a source of the raw data and information that they seek to use as evidence.) There is a range of scientific issues, from solutions to global warming to gene therapy, for which the scientific evidence is still under debate at this writing. By tapping this rich menu of controversy, teachers can help students understand how science evolves while they also sharpen their skills of media analysis.

Teachers can use strategies for explicit teaching to equip students with metacognitive strategies that they can use to analyze and weigh media messages not just in science, but in other disciplines as well—and, ultimately, in their lives beyond school.

8

If You Teach from a Textbook

Literacy is an active phenomenon. Its power lies not in a received ability to read and write, but rather in an individual's capacity to put those skills to work in shaping the course of his or her own life.
—PAULO FREIRE, *PEDAGOGY OF THE OPPRESSED*

Teaching strategies for the new science literacy nestle most easily and comfortably within guided inquiry-based, materials-centered classrooms. However, for a variety of reasons ranging from personal convictions to district policy, many teachers still teach science from a textbook. Those teachers and their students need not forego the benefits of uniting the two disciplines.

Incorporating literacy activities into a textbook-centered classroom demands more from the teacher than from one already using inquiry-oriented materials. Inquiry-based materials often include a range of literacy activities already "built in," such as group discussions using exploratory speech, organized presentations, persuasive arguments, and writing narrative procedures. Textbooks focus on only one form of literacy: reading content. Therefore, teachers in textbook-centered programs usually must make a concerted effort to find (or create) and include a wider range of literacy opportunities for their students. Fortunately, as this chapter shows, many of the same literacy strategies included in inquiry-based materials can be woven into textbook-based science programs with minimal difficulty or inconvenience. (Many of the strategies referred to here are detailed in Chapters 3 through 7.)

If language literacy is a constructive process in which students build upon what they already know to construct new meaning, then the same strategies are not merely useful but, arguably, essential in textbook-based programs. In those programs the printed page, not experience, is students' primary source from which to construct their understandings of science. If students are to master science concepts within that limitation, then they must have ways to move beyond a typical "textbook understanding" of science concepts and to firmly grasp those concepts by using a wider variety of approaches. Literacy strategies can provide those necessary venues.

Also, techniques built around the five areas of literacy—reading, writing, listening, speaking, and media analysis—can be just as effective in the textbook-centered science classroom in stimulating thinking, fostering interactive learning, and cultivating the metacognition skills that mark independent learners. Teachers can use the teaching strategies already outlined, as well as a few new ones, to help students find the deeper conceptual meanings in science and weave those concepts into their personal understanding of the world.

Reading Comprehension

Even if a textbook is the primary source of students' conceptual understanding of science, the sole objective cannot be the memorization of facts. One of the teacher's primary goals also must be that students develop skills that lead to effective processing of information and the ability to weave concepts together to synthesize ideas and make connections from the text to their personal experience and prior knowledge.

Whether in an inquiry-based or textbook-based classroom, students learn those skills from the teacher. In that role, the teacher becomes the students' exemplar of a good reader: it is up to the teacher to let students in on the secrets that good readers use instinctively. **Reciprocal Teaching,** linked to metacognitive **reading comprehension prompts** for students, helps students recognize habit patterns in their reading, replace less effective habits with more effective ones, and become increasingly successful, independent readers.

Reciprocal Teaching strategies help students make sense of their reading by dividing the task into three naturally occurring categories:

- pre-reading activities, in which students form ideas about the structure of the text by looking at the organization of the material, noting chapter titles or headings and subheadings, looking at pictures and graphics, and developing a general "road map" of the material and thus a plan for how to approach it;
- active reading, during which students monitor their own understandings of individual words, passages, information, and ideas

by using such techniques as self-questioning, recognizing ambiguity in the text, and attempting to predict what will follow; and

- post-reading activities, when students check their understanding of the material by evaluating, paraphrasing, and summarizing.

Often, the depth of students' understanding of the information in a science textbook depends on the kinds of questions that are asked not only by the teacher but also by the student. Therefore, the kinds of questions that teachers ask—not just as an instructor but also particularly as a role model of reflective reading—are pivotal in helping students grow in their self-directed comprehension abilities.

For example, perhaps students are reading about the English cholera epidemic of 1854 and Dr. John Snow's investigation of the role that contaminated water played in spreading the disease. The teacher's pre- and post-reading questions posed during Reciprocal Teaching sessions must transcend the "just-the-facts" level—where and when the outbreak occurred, how many people got sick, and so on. Why did some people who drank the tainted water get sick while others did not? What other variables affected a person's chances of contracting the illness? Such questions can lead students in textbook-centered programs to understand that information has more dimensions than textbooks often present. If the teacher's questions relate issues of water quality during the cholera epidemic to today's environmental concerns, students will begin to recognize not only the continuity and evolution of science through time but also how science's continuing themes affect their own lives.

Open-ended questions—about the causes of the epidemic or the differences between a nineteenth-century approach to the outbreak and today's, for example—lead students to expand their view of the material and, thus, their comprehension. A fact question has one correct answer, which narrows students' scope of thought. An open-ended question impels students to expand their thinking by guiding them in using the skills of science and literacy to compare, infer, analyze, and link isolated facts to each other and to broader concepts. Open-ended questions also invite students to entertain a range of possible views and implications of the material so that each individual—with a unique combination of background, experience, knowledge, and learning style—has a greater chance to find personal meaning in it. Reflective questions also entice students to synthesize their ideas and to use the techniques of inference to go beyond the printed word.

If students are to get most of their concepts of science through textbooks, they must learn metacognitive strategies that enable them to read with a purpose, to concentrate, and to develop a personal relationship to the ideas in the reading. Students can progress toward those goals by **writing a list**

of personal questions after previewing a reading. The questions, for which students look for answers while they read, help each student read the material through the lens of a personal interest and create a structure of personal meaning within the textbook material. The personalized nature of the questions also can make it easier for students to retain what they read and to assimilate the new information into their existing knowledge of how the world works.

One of the most important pre-reading questions that students can ask themselves is "What do I already know about this topic?" Realizing that they have a personal background to bring to the reading helps students gain necessary confidence to master new information and assimilate the new information more easily into their existing knowledge of the world.

The multifaceted process of asking and answering reflective questions, and the resulting insights, cultivates in students a deeper understanding of scientific concepts, processes, and issues that underlie mere facts. By finding personal meaning in textbook material—and with the teacher's help in developing metacognitive habits—students can continue to strengthen their comprehension skills.

The **Science Fact Triangle** (p. 151), adapted for science content reading from Buehl's Fact Pyramid literacy technique (Buehl 2001), is designed to help students find and remember the main points and supporting details of a fact-laden, densely worded passage of text.

Teachers do not necessarily expect students to retain for long many of the individual facts they learn from textbooks. Often, it is enough that students understand the main ideas presented in a reading and retain them as part of their working knowledge—ideally, even long after they have forgotten any supporting facts and details. However, too often students have difficulty identifying the main idea of a complex reading: they get lost in the detail and can't "see the forest for the trees." Using the Science Fact Triangle helps students recognize and prioritize the important points in a reading and, therefore, better retain a basic understanding of the material.

The triangle is a simple graphic, a pyramid divided horizontally into three sections. Students can use it in two ways. They can start at the top of the triangle by searching for the reading's main idea, then write a brief statement of it at the apex of the triangle. The triangle's center is then reserved for notes about facts that students need for the short term to identify the reading's main point. At the base, students can note supportive details that reinforce the short-term facts.

Conversely, students can note short-term facts in the center as they read, listing supporting details in the bottom third. Once students have carried out these two essential steps, they then will be able to complete the triangle by listing the main point of the reading at the top.

Teachers also can tailor the labels of the triangle's sections to a specific science reading. For example, if students are reading about the influence of recent changes in the atmosphere's ozone layer on Earth's climate, the teacher could label the center section "evidence of climatic change" and reserve the triangle's base for "expert testimony." From this foundation, students could derive the reading's main theme: that human activity on Earth is altering the ozone layer in ways that have a profound effect on the planet's climate.

By adapting the labels to each specific reading, teachers can use the Science Fact Triangle to guide students to the points in the reading that are important and relevant enough to remember over time. The triangle also can ease students' initial anxiety when confronting complex text.

Guided Imagery

A particularly useful strategy in making textbook material come alive for students by capitalizing on their imaginations is called **guided imagery.**

To introduce the process, teachers can have students work in pairs to become familiar with it. The teacher suggests a range of items that the students can choose from to think about—a particular food, an animal, an earthquake, or a thunderstorm, for example. One student imagines a sensory image based on one of the suggestions and describes it to a partner. The partner then selects another suggested image and describes it to the first student.

To apply the technique to a particular reading, the teacher asks students to preview the material by looking at the headings, the pictures, and the graphics. If students are going to read about microorganisms, for example, after they preview the reading the teacher might suggest that they imagine what that microscopic world is like to live in. The teacher asks students to sit quietly, close their eyes, relax, and breathe deeply. She tells them that they should imagine with all of their senses: sight, sound, touch, smell, even taste if they wish.

Then, to help them enter that world, the teacher can lead them through a short scenario. "Imagine yourself approaching a beach," she might say. "The glare of reflected sunlight blinds you as you approach the water. You feel the warmth of the sun's rays on your back. As you move closer to the water line, you see pelicans bobbing on the surface of the water. In the light, they seem to become a part of the waves and the water. You wonder where they come from and where they go when they are not here. You look down at the warm sand beneath your feet. Then something moves in the sand. As you bend down for a closer look, you discover that small sea creatures have come ashore to make their homes in shells and under the sand. The shells seem to move on their own as the creatures carry them on their backs. You watch them scurrying to find food. You think about these creatures' survival instinct. Where did they come from? How do they survive? What do they eat? You wonder if there are other, even smaller creatures here that you cannot see."

This kind of guided imagery can help students find a personally meaningful entry into a reading about a complex or abstract subject. With such an introduction, students often will continue to generate their own images as they read. This technique is particularly effective in helping visual learners become more actively engaged in written material. For students who have learning difficulties, the mental images sparked by guided imagery can be vivid enough to lure them into the text and to more readily retain the information in the reading.

Issues in the News

Connecting topics in the textbook to **issues in the news** can help students view the text's information as relevant to their own lives. If students are reading about energy and energy sources in their textbooks, teachers can help students find a personal dimension in the material by asking students to bring to class news articles related to energy.

For example, during California's 2001 electricity shortage, one newspaper article pointed out that people can slash electricity consumption by drying their clothes on a clothesline instead of by using an electric dryer. The article raised the ideas of conserving energy and easing the environmental burdens of electricity generation. It also pointed out that the cost of electricity to run the dryer is eighty dollars annually, while the one-time cost of a clothesline can be less than five dollars.

The news connection linking textbook information to everyday life not only can enable students to relate more personally to the reading but also can generate rich discussions that motivate students to dig deeper and learn more as they strengthen their language skills. For example, in some classrooms the article about drying clothes prompted discussions about why people seem reluctant to use clotheslines instead of automatic dryers. The news article noted that hanging out laundry is frowned upon in some communities because it connotes images of slums. However, some people think there is nothing so fresh as the scent of laundry dried outdoors. These discussions show students the ways in which human values impinge on public policy and how the issue of energy conservation can be complicated by individuals' choices and values. Timely issues can enliven a textbook passage and serve as crucial links to science-based writing, speaking, listening, and group interaction.

Graphic Organizers

The Herringbone Graphic, concept mapping, and Venn diagrams (all detailed in Chapter 4) give students a visual way to help them organize the meaning of what they read and apply other comprehension strategies more easily. Graphic organizers are most effective *after* Reciprocal Teaching, when students are able to use the reading comprehension prompts independently.

Writing

In a textbook-centered classroom, **journal writing** can help forge links between textbook passages and students' personal structure of knowledge. Personal journals give students the time and a place to reflect on their understanding of what they have read, conferring personal meaning on the new information and granting it a place of importance in each student's personal repertoire of knowledge.

Open-ended, metacognitive questions, posed by either the teacher or the individual student, can help students focus their attention as they reflect and write: "What new understandings do I have now after completing this reading?" "How can I connect what I just read to something in my life?"

For example, students may be reading a textbook passage about Mendel's experiments with pea plants and the pattern of genetic inheritance that he discovered. They might write in their journals about the ways in which Mendel's discoveries help to explain the pattern of eye color within their families. Again, the journal entries give students a way to relate textbook material to their personal experiences and, in turn, to their personal understanding of the world. Such personal reflections and insights also can lead students to clarify their personal understanding of the material and to discover and articulate exactly what they still do and do not know about a subject. As in speaking, if a student cannot explain a concept clearly in writing, it is likely that the student does not genuinely understand it. Sometimes, the very act of committing ideas to paper helps the student to clarify thoughts. In that way, students' journals can become vehicles for their curiosity to take them beyond the textbook to the concepts of genetic codes, inherited diseases, gene therapy, and cloning, for example.

Group interactive reports

Unlike inquiry-based science, in which group work is an integral part of learning, reading a textbook is silent and solitary. When students work together to craft a group interactive report, they use exploratory speech to test their ideas and understandings after completing their reading. The exchanges are an exceptionally powerful tool that helps individual students clarify their thinking and understanding. Group discussions also provide moral and intellectual support for students who assume that good writing is beyond their capabilities. Writing as a group often demystifies the process of writing for those students by showing them that written material is simply "talking written down."

In small groups, the students discuss the information presented in the reading, what they have learned, what they can infer from it, and what conclusions they can draw. One student serves as a recorder and writes down the group's ideas, while all members of the group use concept mapping (described in Chapter 4) to collect and structure their ideas. The students in each group then work together to write a report, using the Writing Checklist to organize and guide their work. (In some cases, students might want or need to conduct a simple experiment to confirm their inferences or conclusions and collect their own data to strengthen their report.)

In a textbook-based program, what students read is open to their individual interpretations. Differing understandings can crop up in the same classroom. Therefore, every member of the group writing an interactive report must agree with every statement or conclusion included in the report. This mandate for consensus ensures that each student clarifies and confirms an accurate understanding of the facts and ideas the class has studied. (The process also sharpens students' skills in negotiation and collaboration.) By using Chapter 6's performance expectations for speaking, listening, and group interactions, students can shape a collaborative, accurate written or oral report of their work.

Write as You Read Science

This teaching strategy enables students to become more active readers by involving them more personally in the textbook's information. By asking students to identify and jot down key concepts, words, and passages in their reading as they come across them, the teacher gives students a direction and a purpose—an immediate reason to read actively instead of passively. The technique also leads students to become more adept readers by encouraging the kind of internal monologue that good readers develop naturally. It encourages students to distinguish between main themes or ideas and their supporting details. By writing as they read, students also create their own study guides for review and outlines for report writing. Those larger purposes help elevate "reading as usual" to a more active and personal level.

Other writing strategies such as **Structured Note-Taking,** using the **Writing Checklist,** and **creative writing** (all explained in Chapter 5) are just as applicable and useful in a textbook-centered classroom as in an inquiry-based program.

Presentational writing

For use in textbook-based classrooms, strategies for formal writing, such as in narrative procedures and lab reports, may need to be modified. Students whose primary source of information is a textbook will have little experience in designing and conducting experiments, so structuring an investigative procedure might present a challenge for which they are not adequately prepared. On the other hand, writing a first-person procedural narrative can help the student make the link between scientific concepts and personal meaning. Also, breaking down experiments into simple steps and statements— "what I was looking for, how I looked for it, what I found, what it means"— can show students that scientific experiments are not mysterious or difficult tasks.

To gain those benefits for their students, teachers in textbook-centered programs can create investigative scenarios and ask students to write a procedure for addressing the four areas mentioned in the previous paragraph. Students reading about the properties of water already might know that human activities can contaminate an otherwise clean water supply. They can capitalize on that knowledge to devise investigations that reveal how (and how well) water can be cleaned by filtration or sedimentation. In such an activity, students first could test a coffee filter and a laboratory filter to determine which is most effective for screening different materials. They then could conduct an experiment comparing a mixture of water and clay with another of water, clay, and alum to determine which is more effective in removing particles from water. By writing narrative procedures for these activities, and then exchanging the narratives with other students and carrying out others' procedures (even if only in their imaginations or in writing), students sharpen their awareness of the importance of precise language and thorough explanation of details in writing a procedure that others must follow. The experience gives students firsthand experience of how scientists gather evidence, a process essential to the nature and definition of science itself, and one that is hard to genuinely understand by only reading a textbook.

Speaking and Listening

Textbook-centered classrooms tend to be more formal than inquiry-based classrooms. Therefore, the former often do not give students as many (or as varied) opportunities to speak and listen as part of their regular classroom activities. But the formality that often accompanies a textbook program does not necessarily grow from the textbook itself as much as from tradition, culture, and the teacher's choice.

Teachers in textbook-based programs can create opportunities for students to discuss textbook information in small groups. In those groups, students can use exploratory speech to sort through and clarify their understandings and ideas about what they have read. (To start the dialogue, students might read their journal entries to each other.) The very act of articulating their thoughts often helps students better understand information they are struggling to assimilate. Informal discussions give them a venue to try out their ideas and listen to what other students are thinking—and, based upon what they hear, perhaps change or expand their own ideas and understandings. A spontaneous, freewheeling exchange of ideas also enables students to practice using evidence to present and defend their points of view and helps them learn to work collaboratively—an important skill for all students to develop, regardless of the culture and pedagogy of a particular classroom.

Shared Inquiry in Science

These Socratic discussions (outlined in Chapter 6 and in the Appendix) provide excellent opportunities for students to use exploratory speech and to gain experience in using printed materials as evidence to clarify and support their understandings. In addition, the discussions can help students grasp the differences between evidence and inference and to cultivate higher-level thinking skills.

In a textbook-centered classroom, shared inquiry works especially well with supplementary books or materials that explore the concepts and themes of the textbook topic that students are currently studying. When teachers and students have a sturdy platform of information from which to ask open-ended questions and thoroughly investigate them through exploratory speech, the supplementary material infuses a textbook's information with greater life and meaning.

As students participate in exploratory speaking and listening—whether in formal or informal settings—teachers also can demonstrate and emphasize **group interaction skills** and use **Running Records** to monitor students' growth in their use (see Chapter 6).

Whether the teacher uses supplementary materials or a textbook alone, providing frequent sessions in which students can employ exploratory speech enables them to discover the excitement and dynamism of freely sharing and exploring ideas.

Media Analysis

In a textbook-centered program, teachers still can find a steady stream of opportunities to engage their students in a critical analysis of news, information, and media messages.

For example, teachers can clip printed advertisements that make scientific claims that students then can dissect and analyze using the **Media Analysis Checklist** in Chapter 7. Teachers also can compile collections of articles, or ask students to contribute their own, about topics in science from newspapers or news magazines. With issues from human cloning to global warming now on the public agenda, the possibilities for collecting such news stories are better than ever.

Students can use the checklist to analyze journalists' coverage of science to understand the need to view news with a skeptical eye. Often, the most effective way to spot weaknesses in news coverage is to read articles that are months or years old. Subsequent developments, especially in a field as fast-moving as science, frequently will have revealed assumptions or biases in previous "objective" reports. For example, in 1989 public interest groups charged that a chemical called alar, sprayed on apples to regulate their growth, caused cancer. When the report was spread throughout the media, millions of people stopped buying apples and alar was withdrawn from the agrochemical market. Only later was it revealed that the report had not been reviewed by independent experts before its release and that its science was flawed.

By assembling a file of science-related news stories (especially on topics related to those in the textbook) and advertisements over time, teachers who rely on textbooks still can provide students with a rich palette of opportunities to develop the critical skills of media analysis—perhaps even bringing those skills to bear on the textbook itself.

Conclusion: Enriching Literacy in Textbook-Centered Programs

Blending literacy activities into a textbook-based science program demands an extra measure of dedication and work from the teacher. For those inspired to make that commitment, the textbook-centered classroom can provide an array of opportunities for students to engage in literacy activities, not just in reading but also in writing, speaking, listening, and media analysis.

In a textbook-centered classroom, reading necessarily predominates. Therefore, the metacognitive teaching strategies of **Reciprocal Teaching** and Chapter 4's **Reading Comprehension Prompts for Students** fit easily and comfortably and often are the easiest and most effective to introduce.

However, reading typically is a solitary activity that gives textbook-bound students less opportunity to interact with the teacher or with each other. Teachers can relieve the sense of isolation and the tedium of reading a textbook by employing additional strategies such as **Write as You Read Science** and **guided imagery,** formulating **pre-reading questions,** and **discussing and analyzing news articles. Group interactive reports** and **Shared Inquiry in Science** also enrich a textbook-based classroom by enabling students to use exploratory speaking and listening to learn from each other as they gain experience in working together.

9

Fusing Science and Literacy
Practical Steps to Implementation

Anyone who has never made a mistake has never tried anything new.
—ALBERT EINSTEIN

When teachers are asked to fuse science and literacy in their classrooms, typically they raise a series of practical questions. How can I teach two subjects in the time I'm given to teach just one? How can I find effective teaching strategies that combine the two? How much additional training will I need? Will I have to buy new materials? If I do this instead of drilling on the basics, will my students do as well on state-mandated tests?

Such concerns are legitimate. Teachers are rightly skeptical when presented with yet another suggestion for changing their practice. No group is asked more often to alter what it does, and no group is so often left without the support and guidance it needs to make a success of a new method or technique. But many of the teachers asking those questions also are voicing a deeper, unspoken concern: "I'm not sure of the educational value of combining the two and, even if I were, I don't know how to do it."

That fear is only human. Change is inherently difficult and disruptive, even when the person making the change is eager to do so. So often, it is easier to leave things as they are and avoid the trouble, feelings of uncertainty and inadequacy, and risk of failure that any change entails. (To those who do not want to change that which is "not broke," we would suggest that both literacy and science are "broke" when we do not capitalize on the natural synergies between the two disciplines to strengthen them both.)

Those risks can make the insecurity of change seem overwhelming at first. For that reason, those who propose a change in classroom practice are obligated to offer teachers as much information and support as possible to help them understand the benefits of the innovation and adopt it successfully. As part of that necessary information and support, the pages that follow show teachers how many of their colleagues are successfully answering practical concerns about combining science and literacy—including creating necessary, broad-based support structures on which individual teachers can rely. Readers will learn from those who have done it that uniting the two disciplines is not as difficult as many might imagine and can be far more rewarding.

One Teacher's Approach

As director of the Math, Science, and Technology Academy at Chicago's Lake View High School, Marc Siciliano is coaching his ninth graders to read and write science.

The high school was using inquiry-based science materials, "but many of our kids come to school far below grade level, so we had to do something else besides," he says. "That's when we began to focus on incorporating literacy." After initiating a literacy emphasis that helped lagging students improve their science learning, Lake View moved the strategy into its newly created school-within-a-school, which accepts students already working at grade level or higher.

Each week, the academy students in Siciliano's environmental science class write a three-paragraph essay. "If we're talking about population growth in class, the essay assignment might be to explain whether you think human population growth is really a problem or if the world can support more people and we're panicking unnecessarily," he explains. "It's an opportunity for kids to reflect on the world around them as it relates to a science issue and to write about it."

He also gleans science-related news articles each week from newspapers and news websites. He copies each article for his students to read and respond to in another three-paragraph essay, this one following the "issues, evidence, you" format described in Chapter 5. In the first paragraph, the students must identify the thesis or main point of the article. In the second, they list the evidence. "This is the hardest part," Siciliano notes. "It can be hard for kids to identify evidence because they're more used to relying on opinion." In the final paragraph, they react to the issue or relate it to their own lives.

"That's a stretch," he says. "A lot of the issues aren't directly related to kids and their world, so often the articles seem irrelevant to them. This gives them a chance to try to use evidence to make connections to science in the real world."

Students often are slow to respond. Siciliano reports that, at first, he sees many third-paragraph comments such as "This article was boring" or "It didn't relate to me at all." But, he says, "I can see the value over time. We use rubrics so kids know exactly what they have to do to improve. You can see their writing and their connections improve. They learn to look for evidence, they get to a point of being able to recognize it right away, and they can connect to it."

Over time, the effect is measurable. The academy concentrates on communications skills as much as on its subject specialties of math, science, and technology; as a result, freshmen who entered the school at grade level often test one or two levels above grade in their language skills at the end of the year. They also improve as a group in their math and science knowledge.

"It would be self-serving of me to claim that the improvement is because students write essays in my class," he says, laughing, "but there is a tangible result. Reading and writing science contributes to that overall improvement."

How Districts Are Blazing Trails to Success

Districts fusing science and literacy do so in different ways; each designs an approach to fit its unique needs, strengths, and challenges. Yet many of the approaches share common features.

Perhaps the most widespread of those commonalities is that districts joining literacy to science already have adopted activity-based, inquiry-oriented materials. "They incorporate the added emphasis on communication that's absent from most traditional science curriculum materials," Siciliano says.

From that common foundation, districts are building their own structures. In Cambridge, Massachusetts, the science program for elementary and middle schools equips every student with a science notebook to record his or her experiences and understandings. The science curriculum's administrators also created a forty-five-page teachers guide to using the notebooks.

"This helps teachers make the explicit connection between science and literacy," explains Peg LeGendre, one of the district's science staff development teachers. "When we introduced the teachers to the use of the notebooks, the focus of the workshops was to make that connection. The idea was to show teachers exactly how to best use the new tool and help kids organize it to become a resource. Leave a couple of pages blank at the beginning so you can make a table of contents. Number every page. Date each entry. Use pages at the back to create a glossary."

But there is more than clerical work involved. Using students' notebooks as a foundation, the district is developing a multigrade curriculum guide "that includes more science-literacy connections to help teachers move away from purely knowledge-based questions and lead their kids into more activities of synthesis, analysis, and higher-order thinking," LeGendre says. In addition, the group is designing its own formal, written assessment protocols for individual inquiry-based activities and units. For the tests, students will be able to use their notebooks. "The idea is to get away from testing the ability to memorize and to see what students have actually learned," she adds. "We can do that by getting them to use data to answer more probing questions," using their literacy skills to sharpen and articulate their understandings.

The Vista Unified School District north of San Diego, California, has taken a comprehensive approach to the new science literacy using written lab reports in every upper-grade science class. "Science depends on the precise use of words and the ability to communicate to another person what you've done as well as the ability to relate what you do in science to your own life," says chemistry teacher Mike Reeske, chairman of the science department at Vista High School. "A student gives the lab report to other students who then have to actually perform the experiment. That helps them understand in a very graphic way the importance of the clear and precise use of language not just in science, but in any kind of communication."

Students are given written guidelines that show them how to prepare a high-quality lab report. "They always have that guide in front of them," Reeske says. "No matter what science course they're in, the literacy goal of a good lab report is always there."

To make the literacy initiative succeed demands ongoing support for teachers. "When we began, teachers were worried," Reeske admits. "They were thinking, 'I don't have time to do this. This is too much work. It's just one more thing.' We sat down in small groups and said, 'We're going to do this together and learn as we go.' It requires some hand-holding and reassurance, and letting teachers know that everyone's part of the group and no one's in this by themselves." New teachers receive extensive tutoring from their supervising teachers about how to use the lab reports as a learning tool in both disciplines.

"We have to take responsibility for making sure that students have the ability to write, speak, and communicate," he adds. "As science teachers, we have specific ways and materials to do that."

Perhaps one of the most extensive ventures into the new science literacy has been undertaken by the Winston-Salem/Forsyth County School District in North Carolina. It began in earnest to join literacy with science in the mid-1990s.

"Our state has a very high-stakes testing program," explains Dr. Stan Hill, the district's science program manager. "In elementary and middle schools, the testing is done exclusively in math and language arts. That drives what teachers do."

He noticed that, in attempting to improve test scores, more and more teachers were paring back the wider curriculum to gain time to drill students in math, reading, and test-taking tactics. "I knew that if we didn't do something to link science to basic literacy," Hill says, "we weren't going to get any time for science."

He also saw another reason for the initiative. "The biggest complaint from high school teachers," Hill adds, "is that kids don't do well because they can't read well."

Hill and his teachers began by scrapping the district's traditional science materials for kindergarten through eighth grade and adopting new ones based on guided inquiry. The district then paid groups of its classroom teachers to comb through the new materials and identify portions that could be linked to specific science skills named in the state standards. After identifying those links, the teachers wrote lesson planning guides and templates that others could use to fuse science and literacy in their classrooms.

"Now when we conduct professional development for teachers on using these hands-on science materials, we approach it through literacy," Hill says.

In the district's middle schools, teachers work in interdisciplinary teams, and "inquiry-based science materials give something for science teachers to take to their teammates as the basis for an integrated unit," Hill notes. "We have a lot of success with that because the other teachers don't have as much real-world stuff to use. Their kids are reading storybooks or manipulating numbers made up to fit into abstract exercises. The science teacher is the team person who brings the stuff."

Not every teacher needs or values such a prescriptive approach, but it helps minimize the inevitable shock of the new. "If an innovation is of any significance at all, you're going to go through a period where you're lousy at it," he says frankly. "You have to make available to people all of the materials and all of the professional development they need in order to have every chance of success."

None have succeeded more than one of the district's third-grade teachers who began her career as a middle school language arts teacher. When she moved to third grade, she had little interest in science. But, urged by her principal, she learned to use the new inquiry-based science materials and helped draft the district's integrated science and literacy lesson plans—although she never thought she would use them in her own classroom.

But she found the materials enticing, so much so that she volunteered to give up her regular classroom and take on an unusual challenge. The school was opening a new science lab built with money from Title I, the federal remedial reading program. She asked to become the Title I teacher in charge of the lab and began using science as the basis for a remedial reading program.

As part of its broader literacy effort, the school invested ten thousand dollars of a grant in a library of supplementary science books grouped by grade, reading level, and the state science standards that each title addresses. The school provides brief teaching guides for each book. All that a teacher has to do is walk into the book room, choose a title, take the book back to her classroom, and she's ready to use it.

To its professional development calendar, the school also has added time for teachers simply to talk with each other about what they do in class—structured time in which teachers can chat and learn from each other.

The lesson from this particular school: offer teachers comprehensive professional development and materials, give them time to share ideas, and the time and freedom to change. If a school helps its teachers to grow, they will knit science and literacy together naturally.

Teachers' Concerns

Winston-Salem's schools have laid out a template for success in joining science and literacy: providing teachers with the right kinds of materials, explicit strategies, and continuing professional development. However, apart from such resources, teachers have a range of concerns about just what they are getting into when they set out to fuse science and literacy.

How will I have time to teach both science and language skills?

This is among the most common questions that teachers ask when faced with the idea of fusing the two disciplines in one activity or classroom. Those who have done it say that the question itself makes a false assumption.

"Teachers who teach science have been combining the two subjects forever," says Ruth Cashman, a former classroom teacher and now a consultant and adjunct professor of education at Brooklyn College. "One teacher I worked with on combining science and literacy told me, 'I've been doing this for years. I just didn't know it had a name.'" According to Brenda Higa, a middle school science resource teacher with the Seattle school district, "Even though we're not specifically saying that we're doing literacy, when we teach science we are, in fact, emphasizing communication and attendant literacy skills."

Pam Wasserman is the science coordinator in Community School District 24 in Queens, New York. Her district has adopted inquiry-based science materials for most elementary and middle grades. "I can flip through a student book and show teachers that Lesson 22 meets this or that district requirement for literacy," she says. "Teachers don't have to make a connection to literacy because the connection is embedded in science. Teachers are already doing it. They just need to recognize it."

When Vista Unified's Mike Reeske tells teachers that "this is what they've always been doing," he means that "inherent in science is the process of collecting information and presenting it in ways that others can understand." He adds, "All we're doing in talking about connecting science and literacy is formalizing something that's already there."

Indeed, the potential to use literacy strategies to improve students' science skills is implicit in all of science. The challenge is to make the connection explicit. Too many teachers take a less formal approach, assuming that if students read books about science or write in a science notebook, their literacy skills will somehow improve automatically. As Wasserman and Reeske make clear, such assumptions are not enough.

To make the connection explicit, teachers can share metacognitive strategies with students. Teachers also can use performance expectations that make clear to students exactly what good communication in science looks like and explicit teaching strategies designed and chosen to strengthen both disciplines at the same time. Another essential element of making the connection explicit is to use the proper tools to observe and measure students' progress in both areas over time.

Most teachers who invest time to understand the performance expectations and metacognitive strategies discussed earlier, to communicate them to students, and to develop skills in using the expectations and the kinds of teaching strategies outlined in Chapters 3 through 7 find a reward that they report is worth the effort: the additional time required to make explicit the inherent connection between science and language is more than repaid in students' accelerated learning and greater gains in knowledge and skills.

How much professional development will I need in order to succeed at this?

Most teachers and administrators find that they are able to adopt a greater emphasis on literacy in their science programs with no more professional development than they already schedule. However, as the Winston-Salem district's experience indicates, professional development must be set in a context of continuing support.

When California's Vista Unified School District began to adopt inquiry-based materials that placed a greater emphasis on language skills in science than the teachers were used to, the teachers gathered for a week in the summer. They reviewed the materials, shared their classroom practices that were relevant, and talked together about how they could use the materials to do things differently.

"People had time during the summer to make the transition from the old to the new," says Reeske.

The district continues its summer workshops to aid teachers new to the district as well as older teachers making the transition. "The workshops help teachers understand what makes a good lab report, how you keep a science journal, and how kids can use literacy tools generally to become more competent in science," Reeske adds.

"A big problem we're working to overcome among elementary teachers is the idea that 'I don't understand science so I can't teach it,'" says Pam Wasserman in Queens. "To overcome it, we build more and more support under those teachers." Her district offers summer institutes, has circuit-riding teacher-trainers who coach teachers and visit classrooms, and develops "leadership cadres" in schools. The cadres are made up of experienced teachers who can be relieved of classroom duties to help colleagues in their buildings.

The district also has begun to hold professional development sessions in conjunction with communication arts teachers who, in turn, have begun to use science content books in some of their own development sessions.

Will my school's English teachers help me or start a turf battle?

In most cases, language teachers and departments enthusiastically support the union of the disciplines. In Cambridge, Massachusetts, the science program for elementary and middle schools launched a program to strengthen literacy in science by having each student keep a science notebook. For the program's first year, the district's office in charge of early childhood literacy spent seven thousand dollars of its own budget to buy the notebooks for the science department. "That's a seven-thousand-dollar vote of confidence from the language department for this idea," says Peg LeGendre. "There's no question that they understand the significance of what we're trying to do."

When Lake View High School in Chicago convened a faculty conference to discuss ways to strengthen literacy across the curriculum, Marc Siciliano talked about the weekly essays that his students write. "After I made the presentation, English teachers began to suggest different ways I could assess the writing. I want to work more closely with them." Like a growing number of science teachers, Siciliano recognized that language teachers can help their colleagues in science find more precise ways to gauge students' progress. Science teachers then can use those more sophisticated assessment techniques to better help students consciously improve their use of language over time. The usual alternative is to have students complete science-based language exercises without the metacognitive strategies and performance expectations that they need to progress on their own.

It must be acknowledged that mutual cooperation between departments is not a rule without exceptions. "They don't want to have anything to do with us," a science curriculum coordinator in a large urban district says of her counterparts in language arts. "As far as they're concerned, students learn to read by reading storybooks and literature and they don't care that students aren't reading expository text. We're on our own."

Overcoming that reluctance takes time. "In some places, we've had good responses from language teachers but in others it's a work in progress," says Brenda Higa of Seattle. "We find some language arts teachers who don't see the value of combining the two subjects. At the middle school level and above, a number of language arts teachers don't see technical or expository writing as a subject that necessarily needs to be presented. They're more interested in what you would call 'creative writing.'"

In such cases, individual science teachers or administrators can take the lead. Ingrid Thomas-Clark, a science staff developer in Brooklyn's Community School District 18, visits meetings of the language arts department to talk about a possible partnership between the two disciplines. "Very often they're startled by the idea," she says. "Some of them look at me as if I'm crazy." She points out to them that state and city standardized tests in reading are largely based on expository or nonfiction prose and suggests that science content can be the basis of a broader reading program. "I've made some allies who've come over to the cause," she says.

Other science teachers initiate less formal conversations with their counterparts in the language department, broaching the subject of strengthening literacy in science until they find a sympathetic ear. These informal liaisons can initiate discussions that begin to lay the groundwork for more formal, broad-based collaborations over time.

"I always tell new science teachers that, no matter what else you do, make friends with an English teacher," says Kathaleen Burke, a retired science teacher in Buffalo, New York, and now a consultant. In the 1970s, Burke and English teacher Anne Michael struck up a collaboration. "She used science as the content area for teaching language arts, and I used language arts to help kids understand science," Burke explains. When Buffalo opened a science magnet school and teachers were competing for positions there, Burke and Michael applied as a team and were accepted.

"Science teachers I know who have connected with a language teacher work that connection actively," Burke says. "Kids like finding out about the world, so they're more prone to do an English assignment if they can use science as a platform. Science becomes the vehicle the language arts teachers can use to get kids hooked on doing language activities." Both teachers come out ahead—and so do their students.

Will this have to change the way I assess student performance?

The short answer is "perhaps," but probably not as much as teachers might expect.

Many teachers and administrators who have combined science and literacy report little or no difference in the ways in which they measure students' learning. But many of them also use inquiry-based materials, which often come with their own forms of embedded, authentic assessment. The greatest change in teachers' approach to assessment often results from the adoption of those materials, not from infusing science with literacy skills.

"Teachers who are used to giving kids short-answer or Scantron-type tests already are having to find more authentic ways to measure students' learning," says Mike Reeske. "There is no way to measure in depth what kids learn by adding up some numbers from test scores."

As more and more schools move to problem- or project-based instruction, many also adopt authentic, embedded forms of assessment such as portfolios and rubrics. Often, inquiry-based science materials embed a significant literacy component and come with their own forms of assessment that teachers can adopt gradually or adapt to their own grading protocols. Joining literacy to science then can become one more tool to help teachers uncover more accurate ways to discover what students have learned.

It is here that performance expectations can be used not only to guide students but to strengthen other forms of authentic assessment. Rubrics are milestones along the path of learning, but performance expectations can show students the way to navigate from one milestone to the next. By sharing both rubrics and performance expectations with students, teachers not only give students tools that can help them become independent learners but also make the teachers' own tasks of authentic assessment easier.

Again, the key is professional development. In Reeske's district, teachers use rubrics as a significant part of their grading scheme. Each year, faculty members meet for a day to sharpen their skills in using the rubrics. In the morning, the teachers discuss examples of student work to develop a common sense of how an individual assignment should rate on a particular rubric. In the afternoons, the teachers grade assignments and then discuss and critique one another's judgment. Reeske calls it "calibrating" the assessment system.

In Cambridge, where all elementary and middle school science students keep science notebooks, the teachers' guide for the notebooks includes its own assessment plan. Using examples of students' writing, the guide shows teachers how to identify student expressions of science concepts, science process skills, and communication and literacy skills.

"Some teachers have asked their kids to help them develop rubrics," says Cambridge's Peg LeGendre. When students do, "they set a very high standard for themselves" in both literacy skills and science knowledge. One teacher posted the rubric that the students had helped create. "She found that students would write, then look up at the rubric, then go back to their notebooks and edit or elaborate," using language to clarify their ideas about science concepts and information. Explicit performance expectations also enable students to monitor what they do, often in more specific detail than a rubric can. Indeed, combining rubrics, performance expectations, explicit writing strategies and templates that students can use, and explicit teaching strategies is an ideal structure within which students can strengthen their writing abilities.

If I combine literacy and science, will my students learn science better?

No formal assessment tool has been developed to accurately measure authentic improvements in science learning due to increased emphasis on literacy skills in the context of science. However, many teachers who have combined the disciplines have seen evidence that convinces them. Students are able to communicate their ideas and understandings more clearly, so teachers are better able to detect what students know and have learned.

"We have evidence that literacy tools help kids learn science better," says Mike Reeske. "Our evidence comes from standardized test scores like the Stanford 9, where kids show improvement in science. There's also carryover to the English test scores, which improve as well. We also see very graphic improvement from the beginning of the year to the end by looking at students' science journals monthly."

Peg LeGendre reports similar anecdotal evidence. "As we look through the science notebooks, we're noticing that kids' descriptions gradually become more clear," she reports. "They write things that are longer and include a broader range of observations. As they become accustomed to using the notebooks, a number of their skills in both science and language improve."

The improvement was enough to persuade some teachers in lower grades to import discussion or essay questions from the science curriculum into the time reserved for students' writing. "When the teachers did that, they found that the kids were writing more than they had previously," LeGendre says. "The teachers thought that this was because the kids were writing about things that they could actually touch and see and have direct experience with. That made them excited about the subject and gave them a language in their heads that they could then use to write down their experiences with. The teachers saw a big improvement in the writing."

Teachers' comments have been similar in Seattle. While the district's science program can show no data proving student gains due to the combination, "teachers do tell us that they think literacy is helping," says Brenda Higa. "The teachers who are doing it say that their results are positive enough that they're not likely to abandon the new emphasis on literacy."

The teachers report "a new level of richness" in students' science writing, a richness that appears in other classes as well, she adds. "When students are writing or discussing in their other classes, their level of discussion tends to be higher. They use resource materials more effectively, and their thinking and communications skills are better than students in those grades showed in previous years.

"The quality of the writing improves; it's more precise. When they present data, ideas, or arguments, they give more extensive background information and evidence. They're asking questions that carry them to a higher level of thought and performance."

If I combine literacy and science, will my students perform better on high-stakes standardized tests?

According to Pam Wasserman in Queens, "The emphasis on literacy in New York City schools is a sore point with a lot of us because other subjects can be crowded out." But the new emphasis on literacy in science is helping reexpand the curriculum without endangering test scores. "Elementary school teachers see the combination as helping their students achieve district and state standards" in literacy, she says.

Peg LeGendre in Cambridge echoes the comments from a number of administrators whose districts have begun to fuse the two disciplines. "Obviously, this has been a topic at a lot of staff meetings," she says. "Teachers know that our kids definitely need to do more science content reading and more reflecting through writing about science. The teachers definitely see the combination of science and literacy as a way of helping them and their students do better in achieving state standards and performing better on state standardized tests."

It helps in two ways. First, most (and, in some cities and states, all) of the prose selections in standardized language tests are expository or nonfiction. Students used to reading content material critically tend to do better on the tests than students unaccustomed to reading anything other than storybooks.

Second, reflective or exploratory writing helps students synthesize the data and processes they have learned into complete, integrated understandings. The act of writing is in itself a process of reflective thinking in which language is the vehicle of thought; the student is engaged in a dialogue with himself. Students who gradually have developed the skills of reflective writing about content material over the course of an inquiry-oriented science program will not be surprised by test questions asking them to write analytically or reflectively, unlike students who have learned how to answer questions only about storybook plots, characters, and themes.

Encouraging Reluctant Teachers

Teachers' widespread adoption of the new science literacy is incremental, usually a matter of prolonged friendly persuasion in districts where the approach is gaining a foothold.

"I was naive," admits Marc Siciliano at Chicago's Lake View High School. "I thought I could be idealistic and change the world. But there are some very strong teachers here and we have philosophical differences."

Indeed, classroom traditions can keep a strong grip on veteran teachers. "Some teachers in our district are concerned about 'taking kids away' from the science curriculum by having them write," he says. "They believe that the textbook is the bible and it's important that kids know Chapters 1 through 28 and if you only get to Chapter 20, then kids aren't learning enough science."

New teachers often are more amenable to linking science and literacy, in part because they have yet to develop any professional habits or settle into a particular style of teaching. Still, novices—especially science specialists—can be knocked off balance by the fusion of the disciplines.

"They say, 'Isn't this, like, English? I don't remember learning this in Education 101,'" says Kathaleen Burke in Buffalo. "But when they try an activity that combines science and literacy, then they say, 'Aha!' Then they know what to do."

But there is another obstacle to change, one that is often shared by new and experienced teachers alike.

The problem arises because education lacks an experimental culture. As much as teachers are encouraged (or ordered) to adopt new practices, they are not given permission to fail, even for a short while. Perfection is implied as the only acceptable standard. Teachers too often are afraid and ashamed to admit failure or ask for help. Therefore, the fear of failure keeps educators from taking a risk in the first place, even when the risk promises clear benefits for students and teachers alike.

"Even though you see the value of doing something new, you might not do it because you're going to look bad until you know how to do it well," notes Stan Hill in Winston-Salem. "But if you're not willing to go through that discomfort, you don't earn the opportunity to come out the other end as a more powerful, successful teacher. So when people try [to combine science and literacy] and it starts to seem to them like it was a bad idea, at least they know that it's supposed to be that way for a while. It helps when you can show them what it'll be like when they've gone through it."

Offering the kinds of professional support and technical assistance detailed earlier can help teachers through that rough patch. Workshops and institutes, staff development teachers, teaching guides for science-literacy materials, supplemental resources, detailed assessment protocols that incorporate literacy objectives, and time for teachers to talk and work together all are important in easing the transition from the old to the new.

But persuading teachers to step off the edge of the familiar and plunge into a new concept of what teaching science means is a different struggle. The most effective way, many say, is to wait for teachers to decide they are ready.

"You start with the few who are true innovators," says Mike Reeske. "They provide the energy and enthusiasm to pique the interest of other teachers. When the others see that these people are doing it and have support, they'll know they won't be out there by themselves if they do this and they're more likely to come along."

In Reeske's district, over three years, virtually all science teachers enlisted. The latecomers were persuaded by results—seeing that inquiry-based materials that incorporate literacy were helping students learn science better, that students were engaged, "and that they were asking deeper questions and debating with each other," Reeske recalls. "It was a gradual process of people looking at what others were doing and seeing that they liked the result."

For Siciliano, persuasion begins in convincing reluctant teachers of "the importance of application—that science taught out of context doesn't work," he explains.

He notes that many middle and high school teachers he knows who instruct by textbook and drill "are finding that, even though kids know the equations, they don't know what to do with them." If an equation is presented in the form of a question—"How can we dilute the concentration of this acid in the lake down to a safe level?"—the students do not know how to approach the problem even though they have passed tests demonstrating their knowledge of the relevant science facts and formulas.

When teachers see their students unable to apply knowledge outside of a textbook exercise, "it's a great opportunity to talk with them about using literacy in the classroom to teach basic science and its application at the same time. Then, when kids are assessed using real-world problems, it's natural to them instead of something new. It also helps kids remember the science, because it's woven into a story that's relevant to them and shows them that science plays an important role in their daily lives." At that point, students begin to construct a personal understanding of how these equations—which began for them as isolated bits of abstract information—are transformed from something that needs to be memorized, recited, and regurgitated into everyday intellectual tools that can be used to analyze, compare, and synthesize data in order to draw conclusions and make meaningful real-world decisions.

"These teachers have done things their way and they haven't had the success that they're looking for," Siciliano says. "They see what we're doing, they see that we're getting the results that they're not, and they begin to think about doing things in a different way."

The process of friendly persuasion is gradual but, like weather eroding a mountain, the results seem inevitable. "It's a battle," Stan Hill acknowledges. "But even those who haven't adopted this approach see the value in it. They see the results that other teachers are getting—and the value of doing the right thing by their students."

Conclusion: A Framework for Change

Teachers are rightly skeptical when they are asked yet again to change their classroom practices. Teachers venturing into unfamiliar territory are taking calculated risks with their egos, their professional reputations and identities, and their students' outcomes. Educators will succeed at replacing antiquated habits and assumptions with new methods leading to more effective learning only to the degree that they are given a full array of support—relevant and effective materials, sensible assessment tools, professional development, time to work and talk with colleagues, and ongoing technical and personal support. Part of that support involves fostering a professional culture in which perfection is not the only acceptable standard—a culture that welcomes and encourages pedagogical experiments and in which failure is not only to be expected but also forgiven. Indeed, such a culture welcomes failure as a starting point for reflection and growth.

Even with a structure of support in place, an individual teacher cannot—and cannot be expected to—adopt an innovation until that teacher is convinced that the risk of changing is less uncomfortable than clinging to old ways. That balance shifts at different times for different teachers. Some are eager to experiment and reach out for new ideas. Others need to feel water in their shoes before they can bring themselves to step off a sinking ship.

Individual teachers can help ease the transition for their colleagues while schools and districts can ease it for their teachers. The adoption of activity-based, inquiry-oriented materials lays a natural foundation for the more intimate and deliberate connection of literacy to science. Individual teachers can add their own enhancements, such as having students write short essays or read and analyze science-related news reports. Teachers who understand the value of joining literacy to science instruction can share news of their successes with their colleagues. At the same time, schools and districts can gradually build the framework of support that will accommodate more and more teachers as they make the transition.

The process will be gradual, frustratingly so for many educators. But gradual growth ensures a strong root. With persistent encouragement and proper support, almost every teacher can become part of the new science literacy.

10

Making Parents a Vital Part of the New Science Literacy

Parents should understand the goals of school science and the resources necessary to achieve them. They must work with teachers to foster their children's science education.

—NATIONAL SCIENCE EDUCATION STANDARDS

When students enter kindergarten or first grade, many parents become involved in the life of the school. They attend events, confer with teachers, join the schools' parent organizations, and volunteer to help plan or conduct activities and field trips, all because they want to know about and be a part of everything that touches their children's lives there.

But as children rise through the grades, parents' involvement in school declines for a variety of reasons. Parents often report feeling less welcomed in middle and high schools. Also, parents usually are not an adolescent's school companions of choice. (Noted educational innovator Dennis Littky tells of his father appearing at the door of Littky's eighth-grade classroom with the boy's forgotten lunch. "I felt like crawling under the desk," he recalls [ASCD 2000].)

The new approach to science literacy outlined in the previous chapters can help reverse that decline. By using the approach to draw parents into science activities with their children, teachers can make parents part of their children's science learning team and create a new model for a partnership among parents, teachers, and students. This new partnership can not only help parents understand the central role of language in science but also has the power to transform parents from "homework police" into coaches and role models for their children as they take part in science activities infused with literacy.

The new partnership offers four benefits to teachers, parents, and students.

First, by taking part in activities, parents know and better understand what their children are learning in science and how they are being taught. That knowledge better equips parents to support students' growth in both literacy and science.

Second, when parents become a part of their children's science experiences in school, family communication grows stronger. After work, parents are busy with chores and errands; children gravitate toward their friends, television programs, and video games. Family connections can atrophy. Parents of adolescents usually have even more difficulty maintaining a positive dialogue with their children during a time when their children often need their ear the most but are too aloof or "sophisticated" to ask for their guidance. Parents' involvement in their children's science education can create a "neutral zone" in which parents and children can communicate about science. As they become comfortable talking together as coinvestigators, listening to and learning to respect each other's opinions and intelligence, they can find it easier to enter other, more personal arenas once they have established trust and comfort with each other.

Third, teachers—not only parents and students—would reap the rewards of parents' involvement. It has been documented that students do better in school when their parents take part in school activities, know the teachers, and take an interest in what their children are studying (Epstein 1989; Olmscheid 1999).

Fourth, the partnership could create a community of learners focused equally on the processes of science and communication. Such a group could become a model for its neighborhood, town, or city of an effective forum for reflective, evidence-based discussions and information about science-related community and social issues.

SMART Parents

To see what such a partnership can accomplish, we can look at Brooklyn's Community School District 18, a low-income, urban area with a large population of Caribbean immigrants. The district's SMART Parents program (for Science, Math, and Related Technologies) won a three-year grant from the National Science Foundation to create a framework that brings teachers, parents, and students together to learn and communicate about science, math, and technology through language.

In each of the district's twelve elementary and five middle or "intermediate" schools, the program has established a leadership team of parents who volunteer. Those parents attend a two-week summer institute to learn leadership skills as well as concepts in mathematics, science, and technology appropriate to their schools' grade levels. During the school year, the leadership group at each school continues its studies.

Also during the academic year, morning, evening, and Saturday classes for parents (who often bring their children) are conducted by teachers, consultants, and the program's facilitator, a teacher who works full time for the program. In the classes, the parents learn science and mathematics principles as well as techniques for communicating those ideas to their children. Parent groups and leadership teams often organize and conduct workshops in their own schools. The program regularly gathers parents and their children for an event, such as a trip to a science museum or a Saturday science fair at which children and parents can experiment with science ideas through games and puzzles.

The program's administrators have created fourteen different science kits for parents to take home. Packed in small cylinders, each kit has the equipment and information that a family needs to conduct an experiment in a specific topic, such as magnetism or density. The kits also include information about related books, websites, and places to visit. In addition, SMART Parents maintains an extensive lending library of books on related subjects, from which parents borrow extensively. One mother reports borrowing four books every Saturday for her three children; another reads three books each school night with her first-grade son.

"Our parents tell us that the program gives them new things to talk about with their children and new ways of talking with them," reports Barbara Berg, a veteran classroom teacher and curriculum coordinator who now directs SMART Parents. "One parent told me that when the program started, some of the parents thought that the science and math would be too hard and they wouldn't be able to master it. But it hasn't been that way at all. We began with elementary content courses, but found that we needed to offer advanced classes as well because parents wanted to know more."

SMART Parent Pamella Ferrari-Easter says, "I'm having as much fun as my daughter. I have the opportunity to catch up on things I missed out on in school."

The program has helped her learn to use everyday events as a reason to talk about science and math with her child. "We can do it while I'm cooking," she says. They talk about the flavor or texture that each ingredient contributes to a dish or what would happen if this or that one were forgotten. "We also talk about the importance of counting," she adds, "one of these but two of those.

Before SMART Parents, I might not have thought to connect something that ordinary with math and science or to talk about them with her in those terms."

Denise Marks and her family "have always spent time together, but now there are more things for us to do," she says. "Instead of playing card games for the sake of playing cards, now we play card games to learn. We solve math problems and conduct science experiments structured as games. Without the program, we would have approached these things the way we learned them in school, like chalk and talk."

Jennifer Webster agrees. "The program creates new ways to talk with your kids and new things to talk with them about. It's another way to connect."

Adds SMART Parent John White: "It definitely takes kids away from the television and parents away from their newspapers and puts them together so both can talk and learn."

Ruth Cashman, a consultant to the program and an adjunct professor of education at Brooklyn College, recalls, "One mother told me that she and her family used to just walk down the street. She said, 'Now when we walk down the street I have a million things to talk to the children about—the shapes of leaves, the clouds in the sky. My husband says, 'Can't we just walk?' She told him, 'No, I can't do that anymore.'"

The parents' involvement pays dividends in their children's achievement. Denise Marks echoes the comments of several parents. "Because of the skills and materials made available to us through the program, my son has become a keener student," she notes. "He looks at things in a more objective way. He goes through a series of deductions and draws a conclusion. Because of the games we play at home and the methods we use to help him understand, he goes below the surface of a question or an event."

Yvonne Ferraro notes that her son "is now very articulate. Now when he reads, he tends to analyze more and see deeper into the material, beyond surface meanings."

Parents report that SMART Parents gives adults not only concepts and information but also vocabulary and language skills they need to support their children's learning. "If a parent doesn't know what cloning or morphing is, he won't be able to have a good discussion about it with the kids when they see it in science or computer technology or even in a movie," says John White. "The things we do in the program require you to lift your language to a higher level in order to communicate these kinds of ideas to your children."

Jennifer Webster adds, "My son now has the vocabulary. We talk about hypotheses. He knows what variables are."

The program also helps parents learn techniques to keep those discussions lively. "Most people think that a good question is a 'why' question, like 'Why is the sky blue?'," Barbara Berg explains. "But that kind of question doesn't necessarily lead to true inquiry. We model ways that parents can frame questions for their children in the kinds of questions we ask them. This is all about communication, which is why the entire program is closely tied to literacy."

SMART Parents also enables adults to see new roles for themselves in their children's science education. "You're on the inside," says Jennifer Webster, "not on the outside looking in."

According to Yvonne Ferraro, "We know what's happening in the classroom and parents can talk together about what we can do to bridge the gap between school and home."

Espirito Perez says, "[Because of the program] I know exactly where my children should be academically. I know what they're studying and whether they're learning it. Then I can go to the teacher or principal and talk with them in an informed way. In SMART Parents, I'm a voice to be heard, not a voice to be silenced."

Family Science Night

Although it obviously helps, teachers do not need a National Science Foundation grant to use literacy to draw parents into school science programs. For example, to begin this new partnership, teachers can work with parents to create monthly "family science nights"—evenings in which the teacher, students, and their parents gather together to experience science through literacy. These evenings would help parents understand

- that their involvement is not only welcomed by the teacher but essential to their children's success in learning science;
- the central role that literacy plays in science and science education;
- the science principles, concepts, and information that their children are learning;
- what their children are studying at the moment; and
- what they can do to help their children succeed in their science studies.

At the first few meetings, teachers can explain to parents the goals and procedures of issue-oriented, inquiry-based science and the reasons and techniques for fusing science and literacy. Parents could even work through some of the activities, led by their own children or other students. By experiencing the new science literacy, parents are likely to not only support it but also know how to more effectively help their children succeed in their science studies.

The evenings could be culminating activities for common projects. Individual family groups could conduct the same investigation, then on family science nights they could share and compare their results and conclusions. Parents and children would work together to write and present their results. The class group even could publish a record of their work as a newsletter, which can be easily and cheaply done with personal computers.

As a basis for some of the projects, family science groups might focus on science-related issues in their communities. California's 2001 electricity shortage again offers an example. During the shortage, wholesale electricity prices quadrupled in many parts of the state. Rolling blackouts and sharply higher electric bills for consumers were a constant threat. The crisis, unresolved at this writing, gives parents and children a motivation to become "energy stewards" and search—with students in the lead—for ways to cut their consumption, a good idea no matter where one lives.

The search could begin with an informal energy audit, in which families look for ways to curb unnecessary power use such as turning off lights or the television when no one is in the room. They could replace incandescent bulbs with compact fluorescent ones and compute the amount of electricity that each saves per day. Every month, the family could figure what it saved from the month before and set a target for a further reduction the next month. As an added incentive, families could decide to give their student "energy stewards" the amount that the family has saved compared to the same month's electric bill during the previous year—a reward for a job well done.

The results of each household's energy stewardship activities would be shared and compared at family science night get-togethers. The entire group then could collaborate to write and publish a report on their energy-saving efforts, with each family writing about one action it took that was particularly effective. In writing the report, parents and children necessarily would use a full range of literacy skills—reading, writing, listening, speaking, group interaction, and media analysis—and compare their efforts against the performance expectations for each area. The group could make its data available to local news outlets so that others in the area could learn to become energy stewards as well. (News outlets always are looking for good feature story subjects and might decide to publicize the program as well as its data.)

Not every state has an energy shortage for school science groups to take advantage of, but every locale presents scientific issues and challenges suggesting family activities that fuse science and literacy. Parents and students near NASA's Houston campus might study issues related to the permanent manned space station and enlist NASA personnel to help. Groups in northeastern Minnesota could research solutions to environmental problems caused by decades of iron-mining waste dumped on the land and into Lake Superior. Suburban students and their parents could examine the ecology of grass lawns and research plants that might make good substitutes for grass without requiring fertilizing or mowing. Rural students and their parents have the abundance of nature to work with.

Family science groups also could organize stargazing safaris. Most adults and children are fascinated by stars and planets, and scanning them can be an engrossing activity for all involved. Perhaps the best way to begin a stargazing safari is to ask the group to look with the naked eye. A simple star chart can help groups get started identifying the planets and other bodies above their own homes or the schoolyard. Later, groups might make excursions to a planetarium to learn more. The safaris might lead to other means of exploring the sky, such as making telescopes, astrophotography, or studying weather.

The Internet also provides literally a world of activities and resources to choose among. As one example, family science groups can visit a site created and funded by the company Genentech and operated by the National Science Museum. The site includes a page called "The Mystery Spot" that offers a variety of interactive scientific detective stories (⟨*www.accessexcellence.org /AE/mspot*⟩). In "Croak," participants try to determine why a species of frog is disappearing from the local pond; in "The Blackout Syndrome," participants puzzle through a series of symptoms and possible causes to determine why people are getting sick.

"It is our belief that a well-written mystery, with its intriguing characters, puzzles of logic, and leaps of intuition, is a natural way to teach science," the mystery page declares. "We hope that this fictional online story will inspire . . . students to solve the real-life mysteries awaiting them . . . outside the classroom door." That is the essence of inquiry-based learning—and of the new science literacy itself.

Science Journals

Keeping a science journal can be a powerful way to bring a personal meaning to science for elementary students as well as to create bonds between parents and children. For example, children are naturally curious about nature, so teachers and parents might encourage students to use journals to record their observations and questions about the physical world around them.

Parents and teachers can organize "discovery activities" that take students to meadows, wooded areas, or a beach, where they can observe insects, birds, plants, topography, and their own reactions to what they see. Adults can help students develop a knack for observation by suggesting that they look for tracks or other evidence of animals outdoors, for different kinds of birds flying by, or for star formations in the sky. As students explore, teachers and parents can encourage them to use all of their senses—to close their eyes and listen to the sounds of the forest, smell the scent of pines, or feel the different textures of the bark on a variety of trees. Exploration leads students to make their own discoveries about natural phenomena, an essential step in enabling them to create a personal understanding of the world.

To stimulate students' imaginations, teachers can also suggest that they write "empathy stories" in their journals: "If I were a rabbit, my life would be..." or "If I were a tree, I would...." Teachers report that prompting students to make such a personal identification with aspects of nature helps them deepen their connections to the physical world, preparing them better to be future stewards of Earth.

Students' journals can become the repositories of information about what they observed and experienced. As they explore, students can make notes about what they have discovered and draw pictures of things that they cannot find the words to describe. (When students sketch, it is important to remind them not to worry how pretty their pictures are but to concentrate instead on drawing as many details as accurately as they can.)

The journals also serve as places where students reflect on what they have learned—the place where they can use exploratory writing to "hear themselves think." They can be encouraged to describe not only what they have observed but also their thoughts and feelings about their experiences or about what a specific place they have visited means to them.

Students should be encouraged to share those reflections with their parents and with each other. Using exploratory speech to share, and elaborate on, the observations and reflections that they recorded in their journals helps students clarify and expand their thinking. Sharing observations and reflections also enables students to see things through another's eyes and discover details or relationships that they did not observe themselves.

As students write and speak reflectively about their experiences, they often discover deeper personal meanings in them. When their understanding reaches that depth, students typically begin to ask additional questions: Why do plants have leaves? What makes the sky blue? How do birds fly? Teachers then can capitalize on students' newfound motivation by helping them use the Internet or other resources to find answers, or teachers might structure additional lessons or family experiences around those questions.

The Human Side of Science

In another family science activity, parents and children can explore the human dimension of scientific discovery. Because science is a human activity, students and parents need to understand that scientific ideas develop and change over time and can be altered by historical and social contexts. They also need to understand that brilliant scientists are not always "nerds"—that science is done by people with the same feelings, hopes, motivations, and human needs as everyone else.

Teachers and parents can show students that human dimension of science by introducing them to the stories of the men and women of science. Students and their parents can read biographies of scientists that reveal their personal, as well as professional, lives and examine factors in their lives and cultures that influenced their thinking and choices.

Students might be heartened to learn that Albert Einstein was a mediocre student in school or that, as a child, Nobel Prize–winning chemist Glenn Seaborg thought that he was not smart enough to be a scientist. Biographies of Florence Sabin, the first woman to attend John Hopkins Medical School and to be elected to the National Academy of Science, nineteenth-century astronomer Maria Mitchell, and Rachel Carson, who launched the environmental movement, can show students that women have contributed much to scientific knowledge. The stories of African Americans such as George Washington Carver and Benjamin Banneker, an eighteenth-century free black man who was an astronomer, mathematician, and one of the surveyors who helped lay out the design of Washington, D.C., add another dimension to science's human story. If materials are available, parents and students can compile, present, and publish their own biographies of noted scientists. The profile of Glenn Seaborg included in the Appendix provides an example.

After reading a biography, or several grouped around a similar theme, teachers can lead parents and students in shared-inquiry sessions to explore the forces and challenges that motivated scientists and the personal qualities they called upon to make their discoveries. By observing, taking part in, and eventually leading these discussions, parents can arrive at a deeper appreciation of the role that literacy plays in scientific understanding and of the power of such stories and discussions in forging their children's personal understanding of the nature of science. Parents also can see that the discussions cultivate their children's higher-level thinking and communications skills, as well as their abilities to use evidence garnered through literacy skills to derive accurate understandings and interpretations of science concepts and issues.

In addition to reading and discussing biographies, family science groups can invite local scientists to speak about their careers and answer questions about their lives and work. Through the conversations, parents and students would learn more about how scientists do what they do and the personal sense of accomplishment their work gives them. What have been their most satisfying and frustrating moments? How do they decide which questions to pursue? As a group, or as an individual family project, participants then can write an article about, or profile of, a scientist who spoke with them. The articles could be published as an anthology in the family science night newsletter or in a school magazine.

Families also can write creatively together. Parents and students can collaborate to write cinquain or haiku poems based on nature walks they take together. The nature poetry sessions would help students and adults improve their understanding of nature by sharpening their observational skills. The activity also would hone participants' precise use of descriptive language and encourage them to talk together about what they see and what it means in their lives. Indirectly, the activity would increase their awareness of the value of protecting our natural environment and to understand what the poet meant when he said, "To care for the living Earth is to care for ourselves."

Also as a science activity, parents and their children can read poetry to understand how some of the best poets observed and wrote about nature. For example, in the first several lines of Robert Frost's poem "Birches" (1969), we can see excellent examples of what both poets and scientists do: they look closely, think by analogy, focus the analogy very narrowly or expand it to include many things, increase or decrease the analogy's physical scale, and place what they have learned in a larger context that relates to our own lives.

Birches

When I see birches bend to left and right
Across the line of straighter darker trees,
I like to think some boy's been swinging them.
But swinging doesn't bend them down to stay.
Ice storms do that. Often you must have seen them
Loaded with ice on a sunny winter morning
After a rain. They click upon themselves
As the breeze rises, and turn many-colored
As the stir cracks and crazes their enamel.
Soon the sun's warmth makes them shed crystal shells
Shattering and avalanching on the snow crust—
Such heaps of broken glass to sweep away . . .

In this poem, parents and students can see the way in which the precise use of language focuses perception of details and translates their meaning to the reader's own life. When scientists develop a hypothesis or theory or solve a problem, there are stages of analogy, similar to Frost's framework, that often occur first. For example, a scientist will notice that one thing is like another or there is a similarity between two seemingly unconnected patterns. Next, as a poet or scientist contemplates the pattern as it appears and reappears, he wonders if there is a connection after all between them, perhaps a similarity or unity in source. This might serve as the equivalent of a hypothesis. Next, the investigator looks for more examples of the pattern and tries to learn if further observation or others' research supports the connection. Forming a conclusion that the patterns are related is the process of forming a theory. This process unites not only poetry and science but also children and nature.

Parents and educators must remember that "children are born passionately eager to make as much sense as they can of things around them" (Holt 1990). They make sense of things most effectively when they can construct a model—physical, visual, or nothing more elaborate than an analogy in language—that lends personal meaning to an abstract concept or isolated fact. When parents and students view the natural world through the lenses of simile and metaphor, they see relationships, draw inferences, and come to conclusions that imbue the world with personal meanings.

The Personal Connection

Too often, the facts and ideas that children study in school are removed from their daily experience. Family science groups can serve as reflective learning communities in which parents and children can learn to make decisions regarding science-related public and personal issues and to make reasonable trade-offs when confronted with conflicting priorities. Just as a group might focus on a local science-related issue, it can as easily consider questions that confront everyone. What do you think will happen if global warming continues to escalate? What do you think will happen if humans are cloned?

In these reflective learning communities, parents and their children can list their own "big issue" questions to research and discuss. For family science nights, they might decide to invite local experts to speak on these issues and to help them understand the positive and negative aspects, and the sheer complexity, of the questions involved. Such sessions can help students understand the multifaceted effects of technology and the practical, personal, and public policy decisions that technology forces each of us to make in our own lives and for our society.

In another community-oriented activity, students and parents (perhaps with the help of the school's resident technology expert) could create a web page linked to a chat room where some of these questions could be explored in an open community forum. These virtual communities sometimes become powerful engines that inspire people to "think globally and act locally" about crucial, large-scale issues.

Conclusion: The Family Dimension

As parents experience the fusion of language and science, they begin to understand its power to improve students' skills in both areas. When they personally understand the effect of the combination, they are more likely to support it—and, therefore, the science programs in their local schools. By involving parents, educators who teach science can bring families together in a shared activity while also building a wide base of support for this new approach to science education.

The idea of a monthly family science night, a science newsletter that parents and children create and publish, or the other activities suggested here is not intended as a cookbook or a catalog. They are intended only as suggestions to spark teachers' own ideas of ways to draw parents into science teaching and learning through the opportunities that language creates. Among those opportunities is the chance to cultivate an environment in which parents and their children join language and science to create a bridge to shared experiences. Through those experiences, parents can not only understand the power of the union of language and science but also strengthen their relationships with their children.

11

Building Bridges to Literacy in Your Science Program

Even if you have read the chapters in this book and agree with the ideas they suggest, you still might be unsure about just where to start and exactly how to bring literacy into your classroom science program. In creating your personal plan to implement the ideas in this book, you can work the ideas chapter by chapter in a logical progression. This brief summary can serve as your guide through the process.

Chapter 1 discusses the **reciprocal skills that science and literacy share.** This is a fundamental principle not only to use in designing your own classroom program but also to share with your students. They need to be aware of these natural synergies and that by using metacognitive strategies in one discipline, they are strengthening skills in the other. (Students like the idea of learning two things through a single activity—it sounds like less work!)

That awareness can help break down students' artificial mental barriers between the two disciplines. As those barriers weaken, students will begin to understand why their classroom science experiences will be fused with literacy. As a teacher, you can help your students see that learning science, like life itself, is an integrated experience.

Chapter 2 shows **what the union of science and literacy looks like** in an inquiry-based science program. You must carry a similar, though personalized, vision to your own science classes. The vision will be different when seen through the eyes of a teacher of science in a self-contained classroom, an urban middle school science teacher presenting seventh-grade biology, or a physics teacher in a suburban high school.

Think about your classroom—students' range of strengths and weaknesses, the abilities and needs that your students embody, your goals for them, overall grade-level goals, your materials, your philosophy of and approach to teaching science. You must "see" a detailed picture of literacy woven through your science program, and you must preserve that vision if you sincerely want the combination to succeed. You must envision how the fusion of science and literacy will change what you do in curriculum presentation, classroom management, student assessment, and other areas of your work. Such a detailed vision is essential if you are going to be able to troubleshoot all of the pitfalls you might encounter.

Remember that you need not adopt all literacy elements and strategies at once. You might choose to begin with simple techniques in reading or writing, as many of the teachers mentioned in Chapter 9 have done. Experiment and progress at your own pace.

Chapters 3 through 7 provide **detailed performance expectations, student metacognitive strategies,** and **strategies for explicit teaching** for the five areas that constitute literacy. Chapter 4 integrates the three practices for reading science, Chapter 5 for writing science, and Chapter 6 for speaking and listening in science. The three complementary approaches strengthen one another and create a synergy among them that shifts a significant portion of the responsibility for students' learning from teachers to the students themselves.

The **performance expectations** are designed for you to use to help students improve their skills over time, in part by showing students exactly what is expected of them. Therefore, it is essential that students have copies of these expectations and that the expectations are used consistently as the standard of performance each time you give students a task to do in a particular skill area. Students should keep their lists of performance expectations together in a folder or notebook for regular and easy reference.

In introducing the performance expectations to students, you must carefully explain what each expectation means and how students can use them together to grow in literacy skills. If you find the expectations' language too complex for your students, feel free to change the words to make them more accessible.

It is useful to take some class time every so often to have students compare their progress in specific areas of science-related literacy with the relevant expectations, reflect upon their progress, and target ways in which they might be able to do better. You might even want to organize group explorations and "debriefing sessions" for students to share their perceptions of their progress and their plans for improvement. In such sessions, students can create a climate for each other to feel comfortable being honest about their progress and offer each other suggestions for ways to improve. Self-assessment has been shown to be a powerful tool for students to use in groups; it can help them set realistic, yet positive, personal goals based upon feedback from the group.

Student metacognition strategies are the necessary link between performance expectations and strategies for explicit teaching. They are the tools that students can use to help themselves not only achieve the performance standards but become independent, lifelong learners. With these checklists, questions, and prompts in hand, each student can develop a personal understanding of how to continue to monitor and guide his or her own progress.

When introducing a metacognitive strategy to students, you will need to model it thoroughly, explicitly, and often. It is not enough that students are able to repeat the behavior. They also must demonstrate an understanding of why they should use it as well as demonstrate actual benefits from using it. Coaching students to that point will require you to take class time away from science content. However, teachers' experiences indicate consistently that the time you invest now to equip students with metacognitive strategies will be more than repaid later as students learn more quickly and effectively with less effort from you.

The **strategies for explicit teaching** are examples of practical methods you can use to incorporate literacy into your science program. Many of the strategies, such as reciprocal teaching, begin with the teacher modeling the techniques for students. Seeing the techniques in action enables students to more clearly understand what good readers, writers, speakers, and listeners do intuitively when presented with a task.

In modeling metacognitive language strategies, your role as a teacher is to present students with an honest picture of what you are doing—to spontaneously think aloud as you begin the process.

With a reading, for example, the teacher might simply page through the material and muse out loud: "I wonder what this is about? I wonder if I know anything about this? Why do I want to read this? Will I be interested in this topic when I read it?" Through such questions, you help your students develop the habits of mind that good readers use unconsciously. The teacher's modeling prepares students for the independent use of metacognitive strategies such as the reading comprehension prompts for students. After pairing up in buddy groups for moral support and to put them more at ease, students read the assigned passage silently. You then can ask them questions crafted to help them understand the text's meaning and ideas. The questions will help students begin to recognize what aspects or elements of the reading were difficult for them and what they still do not understand. Such self-analysis is an excellent introduction to metacognitive student strategies. Students then can use exploratory oral and written language to formulate their ideas, test them on peers, and clarify and refine them.

In **Chapter 7,** the performance expectations, student metacognition strategies, and explicit teaching strategies for media literacy come together to show you **how to integrate reading, writing, speaking, and listening in science as students analyze media messages.** Media is a filter that selects data and information and then conveys them as written text, spoken passages, and graphic images. Students need the skills of each form of literacy to detect the biases and hidden meanings that the array of media filters introduces when passing along data. By applying explicit teaching strategies such as those included in the chapter, you can help students develop metacognitive habits that will enable them to fulfill the performance expectations for media literacy in science.

Chapter 8 acknowledges that not every teacher has the option of teaching science through inquiry and that many—for a variety of reasons not always of their own choosing—still teach from textbooks. But **metacognition and other literacy strategies still can play a powerful role in textbook-centered programs.** Students who gain most of their science understanding from a textbook have a less well-rounded experience of science, and teachers report that such students are less engaged in learning than students in inquiry-based programs. The reason: they do not have opportunities to construct their understandings through activity-centered experiences. In the chapter, teachers in textbook-centered classrooms will discover how and where they can apply specific literacy strategies and techniques to enrich students' understanding of science, improve their literacy skills, and enliven textbook material so it engages students more effectively.

In **Chapter 9, teachers who are successfully combining science and literacy show you how they are succeeding.** Their experiences shows that the ideas in this book work in real classrooms—and, like a true scientist, I want to present you with the evidence that supports this hypothesis. Therefore, the chapter includes a range of examples of just how and where these ideas are working so you can review the evidence for yourself. We also know that teachers feel more secure about trying new strategies and techniques when they are assured that others already have used them successfully.

Chapter 10 suggests ways that **teachers can use the new science literacy to draw parents into the school science program.** The chapter outlines several creative approaches teachers can employ to entice parents to become involved. When parents become engaged in their children's science education, as they often do through the new science literacy, they can more effectively support their children's work and help them learn. Exploring the environment, meeting scientists in their communities, and developing a variety of ways to express their perceptions and understandings help parents grasp the central role of language in science. When they do, they see the value of the new science literacy and often become its active supporters.

They do so in part because literacy in science gives parents and their children new ways to talk with each other and new things to talk about. It also transforms parents from homework police into coaches and role models for their children. Developing their communication skills in this neutral territory, parents and children then might well find themselves able to venture into more personal and highly charged areas for dialogue, especially between parents and adolescents.

Finally, **the appendix includes detailed lists of performance expectations for teachers and students, explicit teaching strategies, and specific metacognition strategies for students to use in order to help them improve over time.** The lists are there for you to photocopy for your own use and, especially, to share with your students.

Change is a journey and not a destination. Therefore, instead of presenting you with a fixed approach to the new science literacy, we have offered a variety of suggestions and examples accompanied by the hope that you will use them as inspirations or starting points. When it comes to fusing literacy with science, one size definitely does not fit all.

Appendix
Performance Expectations, Student Metacognition Strategies, and Strategies for Explicit Teaching

The appendix contains ready-to-copy lists of student performance expectations, guides to student metacognitive strategies, and aids for explicit teaching strategies for each of the five areas of literacy as detailed in Chapters 4 through 7, reading, writing, speaking and listening, and the critical analysis of media. For ease of use, the order of the material generally mirrors that in the chapters.

145

The performance expectations were created by the author. Many of them were suggested by, and adapted from, literacy standards established by New Standards: Performance Standards and Assessments for the Schools, a joint initiative of the Learning Research and Development Center at the University of Pittsburgh and the National Center for Education and the Economy.

Student Performance Expectations for Reading Comprehension

- Makes accurate interpretations, inferences, conclusions, and real-world connections about the text.

- Supports personal understandings and interpretations of the text with detail and convincing evidence.

- Uses evidence to interpret and apply ideas.

- Compares and contrasts themes and ideas.

- Makes perceptive and well-developed connections among concepts in the reading.

- Identifies and evaluates writing strategies to understand how the author presents a point of view.

Reading Comprehension Prompts for Students

Predicting:

- With a title like this, what is this reading probably about?
- What will happen next? (Turn to your partner and tell what might happen.)

Reflective questioning before reading:

- Why am I reading this?
- Why does the author think I should read this?
- What do I expect to learn from reading this?
- How does this relate to my life?
- What do I already know about this topic?

Reflective questioning after reading:

- What do I still not understand?
- What do I still want to know?
- What specific questions do I still have about this topic?

Evaluating:

- What is the most important idea that the author presents? Why?
- If I were the author, what would I say is the main point I was trying to make?

Paraphrasing or retelling:

- What was the reading about?
- Can I explain to my partner or group, in my own words, the meaning of what I just read?
- (The group or class also can engage in "group retelling," with one student beginning and others picking up where the previous speaker leaves off.)

Summarizing:

- Can I identify all the key concepts from the reading and write a summary using these concepts?

Identifying words and meanings:

- Does that word or passage make sense? Why or why not?
- Can I find something about the passage that can help me make sense of it?
- Do I know something about an unfamiliar word or its context that can help me understand what it means?

Reflecting on reading strategy:

- If I were to read this again, what would I do differently knowing what I know now?
- What helped me most in figuring out what was confusing or unclear?
- What other things could I have done?

Guidelines for Reciprocal Teaching

There are four tasks that make up this strategy:

- question generating
- clarifying the difficult parts
- summarizing
- predicting what the next section will discuss

These are the rules for following the four steps:

Rule for good questions:

They are clear and stand by themselves.

Rule for clarifying:

Look for incomplete information, unclear references, unusual expressions, and words that are difficult or unfamiliar.

Rule for summarizing:

Look for the topic sentence, make up a topic sentence if there is none, and omit what is unimportant.

Rule for predicting:

Use the title and headings, questions in the text if present, and the author's structures of the material, such as references to "two kinds of birds," "four levels of habitat," etc.

Remember to provide students with thoughtful feedback and encouragement when they "play teacher."

Searching for Evidence

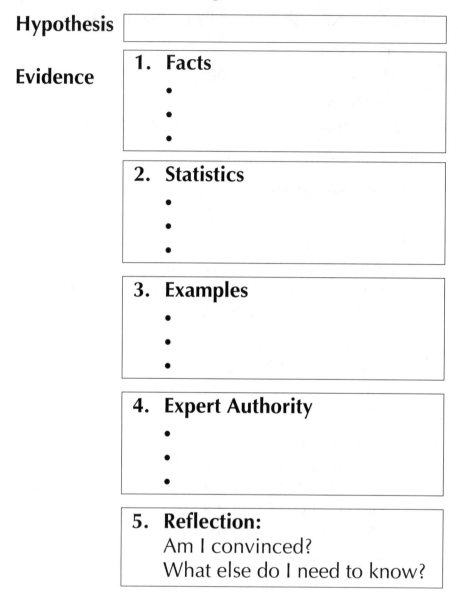

Hypothesis

Evidence

1. Facts
-
-
-

2. Statistics
-
-
-

3. Examples
-
-
-

4. Expert Authority
-
-
-

5. Reflection:
Am I convinced?
What else do I need to know?

Science Fact Triangle

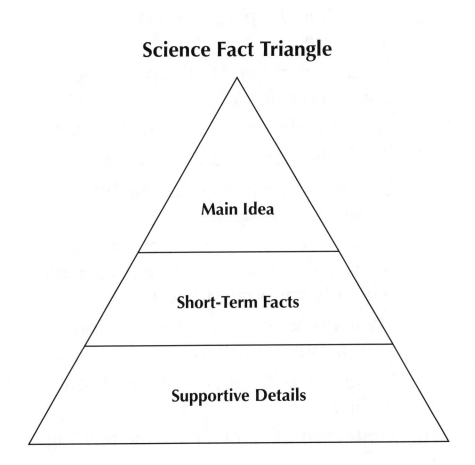

Write as You Read Science: Guidelines for Students

1. Underline the main ideas or topics.
2. Underline the parts you want to remember.
3. Make a mark next to the parts you don't understand.
4. Highlight the parts you find interesting.
5. Circle the parts you agree with.
6. Underline the parts your teacher wants you to know.
7. Write notes about information you want to remember to remind yourself why it is important to you.
8. Write questions about information you do not understand.
9. Write notes about your thoughts and feelings.
10. Write a short summary of the reading.
11. Write definitions of, or sentences with, words you do not know.

Herringbone Graphic

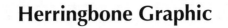

When?

Why?

Did what?

How?

Idea

Who?

Where?

Main

Student Generic Performance Expectations for Writing
• Establishes a context that holds the attention of the reader.
• Develops an overall idea that clearly expresses a personal point of view about the subject.
• Includes appropriate facts and details.
• Leaves out unnecessary and inappropriate information.
• Provides an ending or closing to the writing.

Student Performance Expectations for Exploratory Writing in Science Journals
• Creates reader interest at the beginning, often by describing briefly what the student did.
• Expresses the student's ideas and point of view about what was learned.
• Includes all important facts and details.
• Leaves out all unnecessary and unimportant information.
• Provides an ending or closing.

Student Performance Expectations for Presentational Writing

- Records, organizes, and conveys information accurately.

- Includes relevant details such as scenarios, definitions, and examples.

- Anticipates readers' problems, possible mistakes, and misunderstandings.

- Uses a variety of formatting techniques such as headings and subheadings, logical structures, graphics, and color.

- Writes in a voice consistent with the document's purpose.

- Employs word choices consistent with the document's purpose and appropriate for the intended audience.

Student Performance Expectations for Narrative Procedures and Lab Reports	
Engages the reader.	Do I have an introduction? Do I interest the reader in the procedure? What are my goals for the procedure? Do I want the reader to simply understand the procedure or be able to perform it?
Provides a guide for the procedure that anticipates the reader's needs.	Do I use simple language? Do I define any words that the reader may not know? Do I use enough steps to make the procedure easy to understand? What transitional words do I use to help the reader follow the sequence of the procedure (*first, next, then*)?
Uses appropriate writing strategies.	Do I include enough information for the reader to complete the procedure? Do I arrange the steps in the order in which they should be done?
Includes relevant information.	What information should the reader understand in order to perform the procedure?
Excludes unnecessary information.	Do I write things that are not part of the procedure?
Provides a closing or ending to the writing.	

Writing Narrative Procedures and Lab Reports: A Guide for Students	
What was I looking for?	Describe the research question you were trying to answer or the prediction or hypothesis you were testing.
How did I look for it?	Describe what you did to answer the research question or test the prediction or hypothesis. Include a description of the method and materials you used.
What did I find?	Describe any observations you made and the data you collected.
What does this mean?	Formulate a conclusion based on the data you collected. Discuss your predictions and their accuracy and how well the data supported your hypothesis.

Exploratory Writing and Science Journal Entries: A Guide for Students

When I write in my science journal, I will use these questions to help me focus my ideas.

1. What new ideas or insights do I have now after studying this section?
2. How will I use what I have learned in my everyday life?

When I write in my science journal, I will

- begin my writing by describing briefly what we did;
- express my ideas and point of view about what we learned;
- include all the important facts and details about what we learned;
- leave out all unnecessary and unimportant information; and
- provide a closing to my journal entry.

Structured Note-Taking

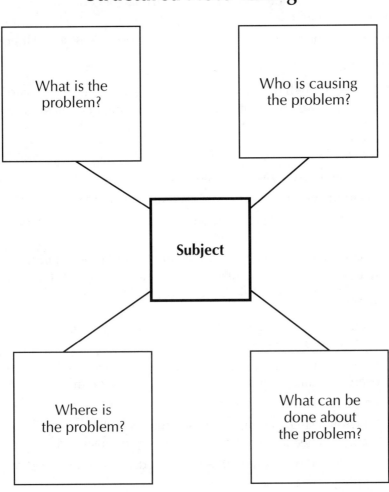

Using the Writing Checklist: A Guide for Students

1. Prewriting:

- I have thought about all the elements I want to include in my writing.
- I brainstormed ideas for my writing using concept mapping or a similar method.
- I made a plan for how the parts of my writing will fit together.

2. Drafting:

- I wrote a rough draft including all of the ideas I brainstormed and anything else I thought of while I was writing that might be important.

3. Revising:

- I checked that my writing makes sense.
- I read my writing in a student reading conference.
- I listened to my peers' suggestions and used those I thought would improve my writing.
- I made at least one change in my draft, taking special care to remove ideas and statements that are not relevant or important.

4. Editing:

- I proofread my work to make sure I used capital letters to begin names and sentences.
- I checked to make sure that I used the right punctuation and that every sentence ends with a period or a question mark.
- I proofread my work for correct spelling.
- If I wrote using a computer, I used the spell-checking and grammar-checking programs to alert me to possible mistakes.
- I exchanged my work with another student for a final reading.

5. Publishing:

- I produced my final draft of the text.
- I illustrated my final draft in any way that was necessary or useful.
- I made my writing available to an audience.

Using the Writing Checklist: A Guide for Teachers

Suggest to students that they staple the checklist (on page 160) into their science folders or another place where it will be easily accessible as a reference. Discuss with students each step in the checklist.

1. Prewriting: Students develop ideas for their writing using brainstorming techniques such as concept mapping. They think about ways to organize and plan their work.

2. Drafting: Each student writes a rough draft, getting down as many ideas as possible. Remind students that revising and editing come later; what is important in this stage is to include anything that might be important. Also, remind students that they will proofread and make spelling and grammatical corrections later, during the editing phase.

3. Revising: In groups of four to six, students take turns constructively critiquing one another's work.

- First, a student reads his work aloud and others in the group give a collective oral summary of what the student has written.
- Second, listeners discuss the strengths of the writing (or compliment the author on some aspect of the work).
- Next, listeners ask questions about any parts of the writing that are unclear.
- Then, listeners make constructive suggestions to improve the writing.
- Finally, authors revise their writing by adding, deleting, or rewriting. They review and reread their writing to make sure that it makes sense.

4. Editing: Students proofread their writing to correct errors in grammar and spelling. If students seem to need extra help, review some simple editing rules, such as those for capitalization and punctuation. Have students meet in pairs to check each other's editing.

5. Publishing: After students write the final draft, they might want to illustrate their work or otherwise enhance the text before others see it. In any case, the point of writing is to share ideas with others. Students can publish a class anthology or a science newsletter for their parents or other students.

Group Interactive Reports:
A Guide for Teachers

1. Before student groups begin work, review the performance expectations for writing. Be sure each group has a copy to refer to.

2. Ensure that group members select one person to record the group's ideas.

3. Remind students that each group member is to contribute ideas to the report and that each member is responsible for encouraging reluctant contributors. (The teacher may need to demonstrate for students some effective ways to do this.)

4. Remind students that before any sentence is included in the report, the recorder must receive agreement from each member of the group.

5. If there are study questions at the end of the activity, they can be used to guide the content of the report.

6. After the groups have completed their rough drafts, review the writing checklist with students to make sure that they understand how to turn the rough draft into a final version.

Group Interactive Reports:
A Guide for Students

1. Select one person to record the group's ideas.

2. All members of the group are to contribute ideas to the report. Each group member is responsible for encouraging those who are reluctant.

3. Before any sentence is included in the report, every member of the group must agree on the sentence.

4. Use study questions in the learning materials as a guide in shaping the report's content.

5. Use the performance expectations for writing as a guide in structuring and drafting the report.

6. After completing the rough draft and consulting with the teacher, use the writing checklist in preparing the report's final draft.

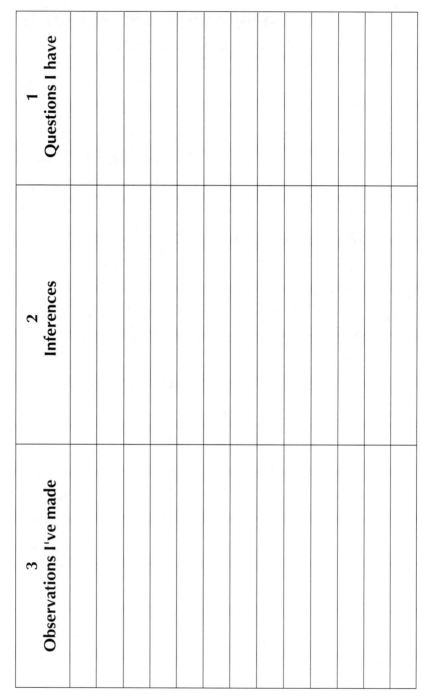

3-2-1

3 Observations I've made	2 Inferences	1 Questions I have

Real Science: Issues, Evidence, and You

1. Issues. What is the article about?

After reading the article, decide what the focus of the article is. That is the issue. There may be one or several issues within an article. The issues may be clear or they may require you to analyze what is written and draw conclusions.

2. Evidence. What facts and expert opinions are given to support and strengthen the issues?

After deciding what the issue is (or issues are), write down the evidence in the article that helps convince you about the issue. In this paragraph, you will state the facts that support the article and reinforce the arguments.

3. You. What does this article mean to you and how does it apply to your life?

This paragraph is the true purpose of the assignment. Once you have identified issues and found evidence to support them, you must react to the issues and the evidence. Give your opinion and focus on yourself. Be creative and explain your feelings and viewpoint about these real-life issues. Use the evidence in the previous paragraph to support your conclusions.

Student Performance Expectations
for Exploratory Speaking and Listening

- Initiates new topics and responds to topics initiated by others.

- Asks relevant questions.

- Responds to questions with appropriate explanation and details.

- Uses language cues to indicate different levels of certainty.

- Confirms understanding by restating or paraphrasing what others have said.

Student Performance Expectations
for Presentational Speaking

- Shapes information to achieve a particular purpose and to appeal to the interests and background knowledge of audience members.

- Shapes content and organization according to its importance and impact.

- Uses notes and other memory aids to structure the presentation.

- Develops several main points relating to a single idea.

- Engages the audience with appropriate verbal cues and eye contact.

- Projects a sense of individuality and personality in selecting, organizing, and presenting material.

Student Performance Expectations for Listening to Presentational Speech

- Takes notes about important information and details.

- Identifies arguments that are illogical, unreasonable, or do not make sense.

- Accurately summarizes the central idea of the speaker's remarks.

- Forms an opinion about the issues under discussion.

Student Performance Expectations for Group Interaction

- Takes turns, adopting and relinquishing tasks and roles appropriately.

- Actively solicits others' comments and opinions.

- Offers own opinions forcefully but without dominating.

- Responds appropriately to comments and questions.

- Volunteers contributions and responds when asked by the teacher or peers.

- Expands on responses when asked to do so and gives group members similar opportunities.

- Is able to use evidence and give reasons in support of opinions expressed.

- Employs group decision-making techniques.

- Works with other group members to divide labor in order to achieve overall group goals efficiently.

Group Interaction: A Guide for Students

1. Do I give others a turn to participate?

2. Do I ask for ideas and comments from others in the group?

3. Do I try not to dominate the conversation?

4. Do I respond to others' ideas and questions?

5. Do I volunteer answers and respond when I am asked a question?

6. Do I try to expand on others' responses and do I allow or encourage others to do so?

7. Do I support my opinions with evidence and reasons?

8. Do I try to use group decision-making processes?

9. Do I try to make sure that the group divides the work?

Running Records Worksheet

Performance Expectations for Group Interaction								
Students	Turn taking	Solicits others' comments	Does not dominate	Responds to others' ideas & questions	Volunteers & responds when asked	Expands on response & allows others to	Supports opinions with reasons	Uses group decision making	Divides labor

Key to Scoring

✓ = Demonstrates this behavior independently most of the time

S = Sometimes demonstrates this behavior independently

R = Demonstrates this behavior only when reminded

N = Does not demonstrate this behavior at all

0 = No opportunity during this activity to demonstrate this behavior

Student Performance Expectations for Using Persuasive Strategies

- Engages the audience by establishing a context, creating a voice, and otherwise creating reader interest.

- Develops a controlling idea that makes a clear and knowledgeable judgment based on evidence.

- Includes appropriate information and arguments to support the main idea.

- Excludes irrelevant information and arguments.

- Anticipates and addresses reader concerns, counterarguments, or other points of view.

- Supports arguments with detailed evidence, citing sources of information as appropriate.

- Provides a summary or closing to the argument, clearly stating conclusions.

Rules for Shared-Inquiry Discussions

1. The teacher is a fellow inquirer, not an instructor, and does not state opinions or evaluate those expressed by students.

2. The teacher or discussion leader asks divergent questions to which there are many "right" answers.

3. Only people who have read the material may take part in the discussion.

4. The discussion covers only the material that everyone has read.

5. Discussion leaders may only ask questions, not answer them.

6. Students sit in a circle and speak directly to one another.

7. Speakers use passages from the text as evidence to support or challenge points of view.

8. No one can cite third-party opinions about the material ("Einstein once wrote about this subject and he says that...") without backing up the outside opinion with evidence from the written material.

9. Teachers or discussion leaders use reflective listening techniques that make students feel comfortable and confident enough to express their ideas.

10. Students save their personal questions until the end of the discussion.

11. Each student may occasionally "pass" when asked to respond to a question (but not too often).

How to Lead a Shared-Inquiry Discussion

1. Lead slowly.

2. Listen carefully to students' comments. Listen to what students mean as well as what they say.

3. If you have trouble remembering the threads of the discussion or who said what, take notes or make a chart that looks like the students' seating arrangement.

4. Encourage students to share ideas with each other, not just with you.

5. Articulate the links between students' ideas as well as the links between their ideas and the divergent question being discussed.

6. Do not be content with short answers. Say to the student, "Tell us more."

7. Turn to the text for evidence to support what a student says.

8. Be open to challenges that students might raise to assumptions you might make in your questions.

9. Make sure that all students contribute.

10. Ask follow-up questions frequently.

11. Do not state your own opinion.

12. Ask divergent questions, not leading questions (see #11).

13. Use reflective listening techniques.

14. Remember that your role as a discussion leader is to be a fellow inquirer, not an instructor.

Student Performance Expectations for Analyzing Media Messages

- Demonstrates an awareness of the presence of media in the daily lives of most people.

- Evaluates the role of media in focusing attention and in forming opinion.

- Determines the presence and role of subliminal messages in a media presentation or entertainment program.

- Analyzes the context for advertising or persuasion that a media presentation creates.

- Uses explicit metacognitive criteria to analyze media messages.

Media Analysis Checklist

1. Who is speaking and what is the speaker's purpose? Who has created, published, presented, or sponsored this message and why?

2. Who is the targeted audience? How can I tell? How is this message tailored to that audience?

3. How unbiased is the information or message?

4. Is the information complete? Does the author present enough information for the audience to make an informed decision?

5. Does the author cite sources of factual information included in the message?

6. What techniques are used to attract or hold my attention?

7. What kinds of words are being used? Is the writer using words chosen to stir emotion or sway ideas?

8. How much information does the writer or sponsor think I already know about this topic?

9. Are values or lifestyles being promoted? What does the message present as being good to own, do, or be? What is promoted as being "not good"?

10. Read between the lines. What is implied?

11. What information or points of view are excluded from the message?

12. Are data, statistics, and evidence presented completely? Does the evidence presented help support the ideas in the article?

Glenn Seaborg: Elements of a Life

Glenn was just a nice, tall, quiet person who worked away at important things.

—NOBEL LAUREATE CHARLES TOWNES

Visitors to the Lawrence Hall of Science at the University of California at Berkeley could not have helped noticing Dr. Glenn T. Seaborg. His lanky, six-foot-three frame tended to stand out in a crowd, and his vitality reflected an uncommonly youthful, generous spirit.

What most visitors wouldn't have known was that this "nice, tall, quiet person" was the co-founder of the Lawrence Hall of Science, its first director, and its chairman from 1984 until his death in February 1999. And that in the course of his life some of the important things he "worked away at" were discovering or co-discovering nine elements including plutonium; discovering a variety of atomic isotopes now used widely in medicine, such as iodine-131, which prolonged the life of his own mother; reconfiguring the periodic table; leading a research team for the top-secret Manhattan Project; and serving with distinction as chairman of the Atomic Energy Commission under presidents Kennedy, Johnson, and Nixon.

For his achievements in the transuranium elements (elements heavier than uranium), Glenn Seaborg was awarded the 1951 Nobel Prize in Chemistry, an honor he shared with Dr. Edwin McMillan. In 1991 he received the National Medal of Science, the nation's highest award for scientific achievement.

Seaborg was a long-time champion of the peaceful uses of atomic energy and an opponent of the testing of nuclear weapons. He helped set the stage for the signing of the Limited Test Ban Treaty in 1963, and he urged president after president to support a comprehensive test ban.

But it is as a popular teacher, university professor, and chairman of the Lawrence Hall of Science that Dr. Seaborg's impact was perhaps most deeply felt by individuals. Even when his schedule was frenetic, crowded with research and administrative duties, he remained accessible to his students and to the public. He took the time to share his love of science. "There is mathematics in music, a kinship of science and poetry in the description of nature, and exquisite form in a molecule," he once said. He also shared with others the lessons and stories of his life.

"I think I was a good student in grammar school, but I had no special scholastic interests," he once said. "[When I entered high school in Los Angeles] my first science course was taught by Dwight Logan Reid, an outstanding teacher. . . . Mr. Reid not only taught chemistry, he preached it. . . . When he lectured, his eyes would light up. I had the feeling, 'Why hasn't someone told me about this before?'"

After finishing high school in June 1929, Seaborg worked as the lone control chemist on the graveyard shift at the Firestone Tire and Rubber Company. The job provided the money that made it "just barely possible," he said, to enroll at the University of California at Los Angeles in the fall of that year.

"I loved physics foremost," he said, "but studied chemistry because chemists could find jobs."

Seaborg described his years in graduate school at Berkeley as being "like a pilgrimage to a scientific Mecca; the chemists and physicists there already legendary. Surrounded by dazzlingly bright students, I was uncertain I could make the grade. But taking heart in Edison's dictum that genius is ninety-nine percent perspiration, I discovered a pedestrian secret of success. I could work harder than most of them. I made a good start toward realizing my ambition to become a nuclear scientist when I completed my graduate thesis on a nuclear physics project, the inelastic scattering of fast neutrons."

Then, on the stormy night of February 23, 1941, in room 307 of Berkeley's Gilman Hall, the 28-year-old scientist led the research team that discovered plutonium. On the following March 28, the world's first sample of plutonium 239—a half-microgram speck later kept in an old cigar box—was shown to be fissionable under bombardment from slow neutrons. This made plutonium 239 the leading candidate to become the explosive ingredient in an atomic bomb—then still only a hypothesis—as well as the potential fuel for nuclear power plants.

"I was a 28-year-old kid and I didn't stop to ruminate about it," Seaborg later recalled. "I didn't think, 'My God, we've changed the history of the world.' I like to say that my biggest discovery is my wife, Helen."

Seaborg was called to the to the University of Chicago to direct the work on the chemical extraction of plutonium from the uranium chain reaction. "We worked twelve hours a day, six days a week. I was hospitalized from exhaustion, but languishing in bed provided no relief. The doctors could do nothing, but finally released me when I made my fever disappear by removing the thermometer when the nurses weren't looking."

After World War Two, Seaborg returned to Berkeley and embarked on "an unmatched period of discovery" during which he isolated eight more elements—more than found by anyone else in history. "When nuclear researchers say 'discover,' they [usually mean] 'synthesize and identify,'" Seaborg noted. "You can't discover something that doesn't exist in nature. [But] none of these elements existed before we synthesized them." For his work, Seaborg shared the 1951 Nobel Prize in Chemistry.

"The task of working with invisible amounts of a new substance—the task of identification—is immensely difficult," Seaborg said. "In one instance, we had only five atoms and a few hours to make a positive identification through chemical analysis. The difficulty can be understood when one realizes that the ink in the dot of an 'i' [on a typewritten page] contains something on the order of a billion atoms."

One January afternoon in 1961, the phone rang in Seaborg's radiation laboratory. "I recognized the Boston accent from the newscasts. President-elect John F. Kennedy wanted to know [if I would] join his administration as head of the Atomic Energy Commission. I said that I needed to think it through. 'Take your time,' he replied. 'I'll call you tomorrow morning.'"

One accomplishment of which he was particularly proud during his early years on the commission was "in connection with the attainment of the Limited Nuclear Test Ban Treaty, which prohibits signatory countries from testing nuclear weapons in the atmosphere, in outer space, or underwater. I served on the Committee of the Principles that hammered out the American position, a compromise between the strongest treaty possible and the demands of our military and congressional hawks."

Of Kennedy, Seaborg later would say that he was "one of the most impressive intellects I have ever met. Even on the esoteric subject of nuclear energy, he responded with penetrating questions reflecting an immediate grasp of the issues. The feeling of youth and energy that pervaded his administration began at the top."

Kennedy's successor was memorable to Seaborg in a different way. "Lyndon Johnson was the most powerful and persuasive personality I ever met," he said. "He towered over others physically and emotionally, his exuberant presence filling the room. When he gave you his full attention, you felt surrounded."

He was less inspired by President Richard Nixon. "Our . . . relationship was prickly from the start. Nixon entered office determined to change systems that had worked well for years, merely for the sake of change. Early on he told me to limit my advice to strictly scientific matters."

When "seaborgium" was officially accepted as the name for element 106 in August 1997, it was the first time an element had been named for a living person. "That's a great honor because that lasts forever. One hundred years from now, or a thousand years from now, it'll still be seaborgium when you'd probably have to look in obscure books to find any references to what I had done."

Seaborg also learned that other honors are less enduring. In 1984, he shared the Great Swedish Heritage award jointly with movie beauty Ann-Margret. At the ceremony, the two were photographed smiling together.

He asked his wife, Helen, to have the picture framed. "I waited a week. Nothing happened. I waited two weeks. Nothing happened. I waited three weeks. Nothing happened. I finally said, 'What's happened to my picture of Ann-Margret?' She said, 'Oh, didn't you know? Nobody's framing those kinds of pictures any more.'"

Seaborg considered cultivating the next generation of scientists to be among the most important work of the field's leaders. "The education of young people in science," he once said, "is at least as important, maybe more so, than the research itself."

That concern is reflected in the advice he wrote in a letter to a young scientist.

"In considering a career in science, you may ask yourself whether you really have the qualifications. You may feel—and many might try to tell you—that you need to be a genius. This is not true," he cautioned the student.

"My advice is this: Do not worry too much about your intelligence, about how you compare with your contemporaries, but concentrate on going as far as possible with the basic endowments nature has given you. Don't underestimate yourself. . . .

". . . If I may judge from my own experience in talking with young people, many lack self-confidence and are somewhat hesitant in visualizing themselves as potentially important scientists. You should have no hesitation at all about doing this. Set yourself a high goal of achievement and exert yourself to advance toward this.

"This age of discovery has [opened] new frontiers in space, medicine, biology, artificial intelligence, new sources of energy—the possibilities are almost limitless. You can be part of it."

(Lawrence Hall of Science 1999)

References

Abell, S. K., and M. Roth. 1992. "Constraints to Teaching Elementary Science: A Case Study of a Science Enthusiast Science Teacher." *Science Education* 76 (6).

Association for Supervision and Curriculum Development (ASCD). 2000. *Education Update* 42 (November).

Bredderman, Ted. 1983. "Effects of Activity-Based Elementary Science on Student Outcomes: A Quantitative Synthesis." *Review of Educational Research* 53 (4).

Buehl, Doug. 2001. *Classroom Strategies for Interactive Learning.* Newark, DE: International Reading Association.

Cherry, Lynne. 1992. *A River Ran Wild.* New York: Harcourt Brace.

Clay, Marie. 1993. *An Observation Survey of Early Literacy Achievement.* Portsmouth, NH: Heinemann.

Daviss, Bennett. 1992. "Deconstructing Television." *Television and Families* 13 (4).

Djerassi, Carl. 1989. *Cantor's Dilemma.* New York: Penguin.

Donovan, Suzanne, John D. Bransford, and James W. Pellegrino, eds. 1999. *How People Learn: Bridging Research and Practice.* Washington, DC: Committee on Learning Research and Educational Practice, National Research Council.

Emmitt, M. T., and J. Pollock. 1991. *Language and Learning: An Introduction for Teaching.* Melbourne: Oxford University Press.

Epstein, J. 1989. "Effects of Teacher Practices of Parental Involvement on Student Achievement in Reading and Math." In *Advances in Reading/Language Research: Literacy Through Family, Community, and School Interaction,* ed. Steven B. Silvern. New York: JAI, 1991.

Fellows, Nancy J. 1994. "A Window into Thinking: Using Student Writing to Understand Conceptual Change in Science Learning." *Journal of Research in Science Teaching* 31 (September).

Frost, Robert. 1969. "Birches." In *The Poetry of Robert Frost,* ed. Edward Lathem. New York: Henry Holt.

Harlen, Wynne. 2000. *Building for Conceptual Understanding in Science.* Berkeley, CA: Lawrence Hall of Science, University of California.

Holdaway, Don. 1979. *The Foundations of Literacy.* New York: Ashton Scholastic.

Holliday, William G. 1994. "The Reading-Science Learning-Writing Connection: Breakthroughs, Barriers, and Promises." *Journal of Research in Science Teaching* 31 (September).

Holt, John. 1990. *Learning All the Time.* New York: Perseus.

Huber, Richard, and Bradford Walker. 1996. "Science Reading Do's and Don'ts." *Science Scope* (September).

Kleinsasser, A., E. Paradis, and R. Stewart. 1992. Perceptions of Novices' Conceptions of Educational Role Models: An Analysis of Narrative Meaning. Paper presented at the annual meeting of the American Educational Research Association, April 1992, San Francisco.

Kovalik, Susan. 1993. *ITI: The Model Integrated Thematic Instruction.* Oak Creek, AZ: Susan Kovalik and Associates.

Lawrence Hall of Science. 1999. "Glenn Seaborg: Elements of a Life." Included in a compilation of Glenn Seaborg's writings on exhibit at the Lawrence Hall of Science on the campus of the University of California at Berkeley. Reprinted by permission.

Learning Research and Development Center at the University of Pittsburgh and the National Center on Education and the Economy. 2000. *New Standards: Performance Standards and Assessments for the Schools.* Pittsburgh: Learning Research and Development Center.

National Research Council. 1996. *National Science Education Standards.* Washington, DC: National Academy Press.

National Training Laboratories. n.d. "The Learning Pyramid." In "Why Use Active Learning?" 2000. The Abilene Christian University Adams Center for Teaching Excellence. Abilene: The Abilene Christian University. Posted at <*www.acu.edu/cte/activelearning/whyuseal2.htm*>.

Olmscheid, Carey. 1999. "Parental Involvement: An Essential Ingredient." ERIC #ED431044. Rockville, MD: Educational Resources and Information Clearinghouse.

Reinhardt, Mary Carson. 2000. "Bridging the Humanities and Science Through Literature." *Currents in Literacy* 1 (2). Cambridge, MA: Hood Children's Literacy Project, Lesley University <*www.lesley.edu /academic_centers/hood/currents*>.

Rowe, Mary Budd. 1996. "Science, Silence, and Sanctions." *Science and Children* (September).

Schoenbach, Ruth, Cynthia Greenleaf, Christine Cziko, and Lori Hurwitz. 1999. *Reading for Understanding: A Guide to Improving Reading in Middle and High School Classrooms.* San Francisco: Jossey-Bass.

Science Education for Public Understanding Program (SEPUP). 1996. *Issues, Evidence, and You.* Ronkonkoma, NY: Lab Aids.

———. 1997. *Chemicals, Health, Environment, and Me (CHEM 2).* Ronkonkoma, NY: Lab Aids.

———. 2000. *Science and Sustainability.* Ronkonkoma, NY: Lab Aids.

———. 2002. "Investigating Groundwater: The Fruitvale Story." Activity Module. Ronkonkoma, NY: Lab Aids.

Scott, Johanna, ed. 1992. *Science and Language Links: Classroom Implications.* Portsmouth, NH: Heinemann.

Thier, Herbert, with Bennett Daviss. 2001. *Materials Development and the Curriculum: A Guided Inquiry Approach.* New York: Teachers College Press.

Thier, Marlene. 1997. *CHEM Toolkit for Curriculum Integration.* In *CHEM: Chemicals, Health, the Environment, and Me.* Berkeley: The Science Education for Public Understanding Program.

———. 2001. Original cinquain.

Thoman, Elizabeth. n.d. "Skills and Strategies for Media Education." Posted at <*www.medialit.org/Readingroom/keyarticles/skillsandstrat.htm*>. Los Angeles: Center for Media Literacy.

Tobin, K., and J. Holman. 1992. "Overcoming Constraints to Effective Elementary Science Teaching." *Science Education* 74.

Vaca, J. L., R. T. Vaca, and M. K. Gove. 1995. *Reading and Learning to Read.* New York: Harper College.

Walker, Barbara. 1992. *Diagnostic Teaching of Reading: Techniques for Instruction and Assessment.* New York: MacMillan.

Wasserstein, Paulette. 2000/2001. "Putting Readers in the Driver's Seat." *Educational Leadership* (December/January).

Wells, Gordon. 1986. *The Meaning Makers: Children Learning Language and Using Language to Learn.* Portsmouth, NH: Heinemann.

Wells, Gordon, and John Nicholls. 1985. *Language and Learning: An Interactional Perspective.* London: Falmer.

Whitten, Eddie. 1997. Original haiku. Reprinted by permission.

Wiggins, Grant, and Jay McTighe. 1998. *Understanding by Design.* Arlington, VA: Association for School and Curriculum Development.

Index